JUNIOR • HIGH • ONLY

GROW UP!

Barbara Varenhorst • Dave Veerman
Jim Kochenburger

David C. Cook Publishing Co.
Elgin, Illinois / Weston, Ontario

Junior Highs Only
Grow Up!

Published by
David C. Cook Publishing Co.
850 N. Grove Ave., Elgin, IL 60120
Cable address: DCCOOK

Illustrations by Don Jones

Design by Matt Key

Printed in U.S.A.

ISBN: 1-55513-496-3

Contents

ABOUT THE AUTHORS

Dr. Barbara Varenhorst
is a counseling psychologist for the Palo Alto, California Unified School District.
In her "Youth Ask Barbara" column in *Youth!* magazine, she answers letters from young people across the United States.
Barbara wrote the "Talking to Kids about the Maturation Process" article for this book.

Dave Veerman
has more than 25 years of youth ministry experience, including serving as National Campus Life Director for Youth for Christ and leading Campus Life JV groups. Currently he is vice president of the Livingstone Corporation, a company devoted to helping Christians and Christian organizations improve their ministry effectiveness.
Dave wrote the "Act My Age?" section (sessions 1-4) of this book.

Jim Kochenburger
is a minister to teenagers and their families at the First Assembly of God in Fort Wayne, Indiana. He has also written several parenting- and youth-related articles.
Jim wrote the "Changing Relationships" and "Raging Hormones" sections (sessions 5-13) of this book.

On Junior Highs Only

Someone with a flair for understatement once said, "Junior high can be a difficult age." (It's quite possible that this same person described King Kong as "a large monkey.")

Junior high is a time of tremendous upheaval and uncertainty. In a very short period of time, kids experience radical change in their physical appearance, are forced to deal with emotions and feelings they've never encountered before, and are faced with an entirely new set of temptations and problems.

Perhaps no other age group has as much need for guidance and direction as junior highers.

With that in mind, we've created "Junior Highs Only."

Written by youth workers with "in-the-trenches" junior high experience, "Junior Highs Only" addresses the specific needs of junior highers—at a level they can understand and relate to. Each biblically based session was written with the learning capabilities and boredom-tolerance levels of junior highers in mind.

We've also remembered that today's junior highers face issues that yesterday's kids didn't face until high school. So in addition to the "usual" topics—facing everyday fears at school, feeling comfortable with one's rapidly changing body, etc.—"Junior Highs Only" addresses the dangers of experimenting with sex, drugs, alcohol, the occult, and more.

Use "Junior Highs Only" for the liveliest Sunday school classes you've had in a long time—or add one of the "Youth Group" options for an evening meeting. Check out the "Adapting the Session for Sixth Graders" sections if you have a group of middle schoolers.

Use one session to address a specific, immediate need in your group, or use one of the four- or five-session sections of the book for a month. Or use the entire book for 13 weeks. You've got plenty of options!

We hope the exciting activities, interesting Bible studies, and practical application of "Junior Highs Only" will provide valuable guidance and direction for your confused, eager, impatient, full-of-potential junior highers.

— Randy Southern, Series Editor

Introduction

Talking to Kids about the Maturation Process

The challenges connected with talking to kids about the maturation process are created by the maturation process itself. You will find no greater diversity exists in any age group than you find among junior highers, in terms of size and shapes, social skills, thinking abilities, vocabularies, and emotional highs and lows.

Looking around your group, you will probably see some kids jostling and hitting, grabbing others' possessions to get attention like children, while others look and behave like high school students, covering up their uncertainties and shyness with a veneer of confidence.

Junior high kids giggle, laugh at one another for no particular reason, and, having discovered the word "love," apply it to any person or thing they vaguely like. Some know a little about the physical elements of sex, but almost nothing of the emotional and spiritual aspects. Most still think concretely, dealing only with the specifics of the present, while some have begun maturing intellectually, awakening to peer opinions, and the resulting pain of self-conscious awkwardness.

This diversity *is* a challenge to anyone who talks to early adolescents about growing up, especially with a combined group of boys and girls. Yet there are no kids more open to learning about themselves, despite how well they hide this eagerness, than junior highers. And they *do* want—and need—to do this with peers of the opposite sex, especially when the topic of physical growth is covered. As one seventh-grade boy said to me, "I know about *my* body, but I don't know about girls' bodies, and I need to know this."

Kids are confused about all the changes that are occurring. They don't know what to expect, why they feel and act the way they do; and they worry about whether they're normal. They need someone who can calm them down, provide assurance, and equip them with a road map of what lies ahead. If you exhibit patience and understanding and answer questions honestly and respectfully, your wiggly group members will settle down gradually, begin to trust you, and reward you with their growth.

Key Pointers about the Maturation Process

Most instruction given to young people about what happens as they grow up is focused primarily on their physical maturation. As important as this area is—because it triggers changes in how a child is treated—there are other areas of growth that are equally, if not more important in helping children through this volcanic period of life.

Intellectual growth—the process which changes young people's thinking about themselves, others, and the world around them—perhaps has a more powerful effect on their lives than puberty. Because this growth is less visible, it is often ignored, misunderstood, and confusing to the kids themselves. This "revolution" in their thinking often begins before the onset of puberty, and is not completely mature until young adulthood.

It is this new ability that makes them critical and self-conscious about the changes in their bodies, that makes them fear being different, that occasionally makes them rude, and that introduces the frequently asked question, "Who am I?" Kids need to have this explained to them, even though some may not comprehend all that it means.

Understanding this cognitive change that is happening to your group members can serve as a guide in planning your approaches to the sessions. Talking "at" your group members should be kept to a minimum, since their attention span is quite limited. Varying a session with individual and group activities, followed by *teaching* group discussions is an effective approach.

Junior highers often sound as though they have more knowledge and sophistication than their teachers and parents, especially when it comes to discussing sex. This veneer often shuts adults up, or leads them to assume that kids have more knowledge than the kids actually have. I never assume such knowledge, but explore what they *do* know by asking questions.

I strongly recommend the "*asking* first and *telling* later" approach. With each of the topics in this book, begin by asking group members for their understanding of the topics. Then, based on their answers, weave into the session corrections of any misunderstandings they have, or additions that you want them to consider. These "lectures" often are more effective because the kids first had a chance to provide their thoughts and ideas, and thus will be more open to consider other perspectives.

The area of emotional growth, so important to young people's understanding of themselves, should never be neglected. Kids don't realize that when hormones begin pouring into their system, it's not just bodies that are changed—it's their emotional awareness and response to life as well. Without this maturity, no one would ever experience the joys and depths of adult emotions, nor understand true compassion, love, and commitment that give meaning to life. But for the teenager, it causes problems: mood swings, irritability, crushes, and the roller coaster of likes and dislikes, pain and pleasure. Once, when teaching a course on human sexuality to seventh and eighth graders, I explained about emotional development. A girl spoke up, looking as though a light had just dawned in her mind, and she said, "Is *that* what makes me feel the way I do?" Then she sat in quiet reflection during the remainder of the class.

Discussion of emotional development leads to discussion of its impact on boy-girl relationships, and eventually to the more intimate discussion of sexual relationships. Kids are often baffled that playmates they had taken for granted suddenly make them feel awkward and uncomfortable.

They wonder why they blush, get tongue-tied, or feel strange movements in their stomachs when they are around certain members of the opposite sex. They ask why deciding to become boyfriends and girlfriends with someone who was a comfortable friend makes them distant from one another, searching for things to say, and less free in suggesting things they could do together.

Nor do they understand that sex appeal—becoming attractive to the opposite sex—is a function of one's unfolding emotional maturity, activated on a time schedule unique to each individual. Using examples from your own experience, as well as experiences you know some of your group members are having, explain what is happening and why. Their ears will be open, and their attention will be prepared to move on to the discussion of sexual issues which follow.

As I have worked with junior high youth, I have found certain things that must be established and different approaches that are effective in talking to them about personal issues. An atmosphere of trust and comfort must be established, tested by how you protect the dignity of each child. The content must be meaningful, in touch with what they are thinking, feeling, and experiencing. The methods need to be in tune with their capabilities, but challenging to their growth. You as a leader need to enjoy this age group and feel comfortable in sharing openly and honestly when it is appropriate.

Growing up Spiritually

The junior high years are the most fruitful time for nurturing the seeds of spiritual growth. The gradual awakening of kids' awareness to things around them, their beginning ability to anticipate the future, their penetrating questions, and their exploration of values lead them to explore their relationships with God.

This book is designed to equip you to nurture junior highers' spiritual growth as well as to help them grow in knowledge about themselves and others. You will see that the challenges of talking to kids about maturation are both rewarding and a fulfillment of service to God, who has given you this sacred opportunity.

— Barbara Varenhorst

Session 1

Junior high is a time of transition between "early" and "middle" adolescence. Children are becoming "young people," and they are changing in every area of life. Some of these changes are exhilarating and exciting, like having more freedom and learning new skills. But many of the changes can be frustrating and difficult, like gaining new responsibilities, going up and down emotionally, and experiencing dramatic physical growth. A common response to these changes is fear. Most junior highers feel intensely alone (thinking that only they have these struggles), and they wonder how they will cope in the future. The first step in helping calm their fears is to let them know that their changes and feelings are normal—most kids their age are going through the same things. It will also be helpful to let them know that God is with them in their changes and increased responsibilities. He will give them wisdom and strength to handle whatever comes.

It's Not So Bad

[Addressing the Fear of Growing Up]

What You Want to Do

- Help ease kids' minds concerning the advent of increased responsibilities;
- Help kids understand that God will supply sufficient wisdom and ability to handle increased responsibilities as they grow and mature.

Where You'll Find Help

- Proverbs 13:20
- Luke 2:52
- Romans 8:28
- I Corinthians 10:13
- Philippians 1:6; 2:12, 13
- James 1:2-8

What You'll Need

- Bibles
- Pencils
- Copies of "Changes" (Student Sheet 1-A)
- Copies of "Future Shock" (Student Sheet 1-B)
- Baby pictures of group members mounted on cardboard
- Index cards

1

You Must Have Been a Beautiful Baby

During the week, collect baby (or toddler) pictures of group members from their parents, but don't let anyone in the group know that you have the pictures. Try to have a picture of everyone in the group, including yourself. Mount the pictures on individual pieces of cardboard and number them. (Note: Slides would be even better, if you can get them and if you have the projection equipment.)

Distribute pencils and index cards. Have the group write the numbers 1-? (depending on how many pictures you have) down the left-hand side of the cards. Then pass out the pictures, starting them at both sides of the room. Tell group members to look at each picture and then write the name of the person on the appropriate line on their cards. Keep the pictures moving and make sure that everyone has seen all the pictures at least once.

Collect the pictures. Display them one at a time, revealing the correct identities as you go. (NOTE: Don't allow anyone to make fun of anyone else. Use this to affirm kids—talk about the beautiful smile, how cute the person is, etc.) See who had the most correct answers. Collect the cards, but have them keep the pencils.

Ask: **How were you able to figure out whose pictures those were?** (Physical characteristics: eyes, nose, chin, etc.)

Which pictures were the toughest to figure out? Why?

In what ways have those babies changed?

Say something like: **Obviously we've all changed a lot since we were little babies. And it's a good thing we have. How would you like to still look like your baby picture? Change is a part of life. It will be interesting to see how much you change in the next five or six years. Wouldn't it be fun to have pictures now of what you'll look like then?**

2

Changes

Distribute copies of "Changes" (Student Sheet 1-A). Say something like: **By looking at the baby pictures, we were able to see some of the physical changes that we've experienced. But we've changed in other ways, too. Take a couple of minutes to fill out this worksheet. Then we'll compare notes to see how else we've changed.**

Allow a few minutes for everyone to fill out the sheets. Then compare the answers for "Favorite Song," "Favorite Food," "Favorite Snack," and "Favorite TV Show." It should be interesting to see how your group members' tastes have changed. Next, see what they wrote for the last category, "Favorite Adult (besides parents)."

Ask your group members how they feel about these changes. They probably haven't given any of them much thought because changes in those areas seem natural and are no big deal. Explain again how change is a part of life, especially during the first twenty years or so.

3 Future Shock

Discuss other changes that will occur in the following areas: physical, social, mental, spiritual, and responsibilities. Write those categories on the board and jot down group members' answers after each one.

The answers will probably include: physical—size, looks, sexual feelings, pimples; social—friends, popularity, independence, personality; mental—grades, thoughts, ideas, goals; spiritual—church, guilt, understanding the Bible, relationship with God; responsibilities—taking care of younger brothers and sisters, earning own spending money, doing more work around the house, saving money for college.

Say something like: **Changes can be cute and even funny, like the difference between our baby pictures and the way we look now. Changes can be interesting, like those we wrote on our "Changes" worksheets. But changes can also be scary, like some of these we just put on the board.**

Take "friends," for example. Sometimes in junior high, our friends change. Even our closest friend may begin to hang around with another group of kids—and that can hurt. It could also cause us to be afraid that *all* our friends will change. Or, what about physical changes? Some kids see their feet begin to grow and wonder if the rest of their body will ever catch up. Others think that they're too tall—or too short—and they are afraid of becoming some sort of freak. Or some may just be afraid of having increased responsibilities as they grow older, like having to study more in school. If we're honest, probably all of us would admit that we have fears about some of the changes in our lives.

Distribute "Future Shock" (Student Sheet 1-B) and have group members fill in the first two columns. In the column labeled "Change," they should write one change in any area that is causing (or might cause) them fear. Then, in the column labeled "Fear," they should write what they are (or could be) afraid of. The column labeled "Verses" should be left blank.

Encourage everyone to fill in every blank in the first two columns. Tell group members to be honest in their answers and to keep their papers private. No one else should see their sheets, and you won't collect them or discuss what they wrote. Let them know, however, that if they have questions, you and/or your assistants will be very willing to help.

After a few minutes, have everyone stop writing. Then say something like: **As I said earlier, these fears are normal. Everyone has some fears about what the changes in his or her life may bring. But the good news is that we don't**

have to face these changes and the future alone. God has given us His Word, the Bible, and He has promised to be with us—that's what we'll look at next.

4 Check It Out

Have group members take out their Bibles and look up the following passages (write the references on the board):

James 1:2-8
Proverbs 13:20
Philippians 1:6
I Corinthians 10:13
Philippians 2:12, 13

Then have group members write these verses in the appropriate squares in the column labeled "Verses" on Student Sheet 1-B.

After a few minutes, have everyone share where he or she put the verses and why. The verses will probably fit into these categories: physical—I Corinthians 10:13; social—Proverbs 13:20; mental—James 1:2-8; spiritual—Philippians 1:6; responsibilities—Philippians 2:12, 13.

Discuss why they placed the verses where they did.

5 Working in Us

Close by emphasizing the truths in the following passages:

Luke 2:52—Jesus grew and changed also. He understands what kids are going through.

Romans 8:28—God will work everything for good, even the dreaded changes in our lives, if we trust Him and let Him work.

Philippians 2:12, 13—As we change, God works in us, helping us want to do what is right, changing our desires, and then giving us the power to do it.

I Corinthians 10:13—Although we will be tempted as we grow and mature, God will be with us through the temptations, protecting us and providing a way out of them.

James 1:2-8—God's wisdom is always available. When we don't know what to do or which way to turn, we can ask Him.

6

Taking Action

Instruct your group members to make it a point to talk to God *every day* in the coming week about their "change" fears.

Then close the session in prayer, thanking God that He is available to listen to and help us overcome our fears.

Options for Use in Youth Group

Child's Play

Begin the meeting with a number of children's activities. Have group members form two teams and compete to see which team can complete the activities fastest.

One activity you might use is "Ring around the Rosey." In this game, everyone on a team joins hands and walks around in a circle, saying, "Ring around the rosey, a pocketful of posies, ashes, ashes, we all fall down." On "we all fall down," everyone falls to the ground.

Afterward, ask volunteers to tell about their favorite childhood games.

Dueling Ditties

Have group members form two teams. Instruct them to say or sing, one team at a time, the first few lines of a nursery rhyme. The teams go back and forth, and each time must repeat a rhyme that hasn't been used. The first team to repeat or to take too long to think of a nursery rhyme loses.

Adapting the Session for Sixth Graders

Most of the session can be used effectively with sixth graders as it is written. You may need to keep an eye on them when you distribute student sheets. Some kids may be tempted to make paper airplanes, fold the sheets into interesting shapes, or poke holes in them. You may want to walk around the room to make sure group members fill out the student sheets.

Changes

	0-5 years old	5-10 years old	Now
Favorite Song			
Favorite Food			
Favorite Snack			
Favorite TV Show			
Favorite Adult (besides parent)			

FUTURE Shock

	Change	Fear	Verses
Physical			
Social			
Mental			
Spiritual			
Responsibilities			

Session 2

Because of the dramatic changes in all areas of their lives, growing up doesn't seem like a very exciting prospect to most early adolescents as they try to navigate the difficult passage into maturity. Their lives seem to be getting increasingly complicated as they struggle with learning new skills, dealing with new responsibilities, and thinking in terms of ideas instead of just facts. It is important, then, to help these young people see life from a positive perspective, to see that there are many benefits to growing older and maturing. Among the benefits: they will be able to learn more, experience more, and do more on their own, and they will be able relate to God on a deeper level.

Growing Up Is a Many-Splendored Thing

[The Joys of Maturity]

What You Want to Do

- Help kids understand that many benefits and increased privileges come with growing older and maturing;
- Help kids recognize the opportunity they have to know and relate to God on a deeper level as they mature.

Where You'll Find Help

- I Corinthians 9:24-27; 13:11
- Philippians 3:12-14
- I Timothy 4:7-10
- II Timothy 4:7, 8

What You'll Need

- Bibles
- Pencils
- Copies of "As a Child" (Student Sheet 2-A)
- Copies of "Timelines" (Student Sheet 2-B)
- Noisemakers, toy instruments, blocks, rattles, etc. for "Rhythm Band"
- Crayons

1 Rhythm Band

Begin this session by saying something like: **I want you to do something that you probably haven't done for many years—play in a rhythm band. I want to see if you still have the talent.** Then pass out various noisemakers, toy instruments, blocks, rattles, and so forth. Tell those who have the toy instruments to carry the tune while the others provide the rhythm. Have everyone play a familiar song together (e.g., "Mary Had a Little Lamb," "America the Beautiful," "The Battle Hymn of the Republic," "Happy Birthday," etc.). Give your "more advanced" musicians balloons that they can inflate and use as noisemakers by slowly letting air escape.

When the group is finished playing the song, give individuals an opportunity to form their own small musical groups with two or three other people and play a current pop song. Allow time for three or four such groups to perform.

Afterward, collect all the instruments and noisemakers.

2 As a Child

Distribute copies of "As a Child" (Student Sheet 2-A) and crayons. Instruct group members to follow the directions on the sheet. After a few minutes, collect the crayons and have kids display and explain what they have drawn. Look especially for what they drew as "childish ways."

Afterward, say something like: **We're looking at how we've changed over the years. Changes are happening right now in our bodies and minds. These changes are normal; we have nothing to fear, and God is with us in all of them. Today, we'll be seeing how these changes can be exciting and good. It was interesting to see what you drew for "childish ways" on the student sheets. Those kinds of things—baby food, dolls, tricycles, and so forth—we've put behind us as we've moved on to other, more grown-up toys and activities.**

But if those are "childish ways," what are "adultish ways"? Discuss this briefly.

Timelines

Then say something like: **The word that is used to describe the process of going from child to adult is "maturation"—becoming mature. Let's face it, there's a lot of difference between a little child and an adult. And getting from one stage to another involves quite a few changes. Right now you are in the middle of this process—in transition. If we could diagram this process, it might look like this.** Draw a horizontal line on the board with an arrowhead at the right end.

This is a timeline. At the far left end, we have a baby, and at the far right, an adult. Now, let's look at this person's life in a very specific area—swimming. Way at the left end, we could write, "Splashes in the tub." Write each of these phrases as you give them, along the timeline at the appropriate places.

The next stage might be "Plays in the wading pool." Next, we could write, "Takes swimming lessons." And a few years later, we might add, "Joins a swim team." Eventually, we may even want to write, "Makes Olympic swimming team." The point is, there's a progression in the child's relationship with water. And tons of changes had to occur to transform the helpless baby into an Olympic champion.

Of course, not everyone will be in the Olympics, and that may not be your goal. But whatever the goal, change is an important part of getting from here to there.

Distribute "Timelines" (Student Sheet 2-B). Say: **The Bible talks about goals. On this sheet there are timelines, similar to the one that I put on the board. Read each passage. Then write the goal at the right end of the line, and write the steps and changes that might have to happen for a person to reach that goal.** Encourage group members to look not only at the passages listed, but at the verses that surround each passage, too.

Possible goals could include:

I Corinthians 9:24-27—God's prize, a crown that will last forever;

Philippians 3:12-14—God's prize in heaven;

I Timothy 4:7-10—godliness;

II Timothy 4:7, 8—crown of righteousness.

After everyone has finished, ask for volunteers to share their answers for the goal column. Then discuss what they wrote for the "process" on each line.

Say something like: **In each of these passages, the Apostle Paul was talking about his life. This is the same man who said that he had "put childish ways behind" him. Paul certainly had goals for his life—to be closer to God, to live the way God wanted, to be faithful to Christ, to gain an eternal crown from God, and so forth.**

We don't know everything about Paul, but he began life just like you and me—as a baby. Then he was a toddler and a young child. He went to school and learned. He grew physically, mentally, socially, and spiritually. Later, as an adult, he studied very hard to be a very religious person. He spent time

trying to capture and kill people who believed in Jesus.

But then there was another change in Paul's life—he met Christ and became Christ's follower. That experience put Paul on a new life track—moving toward reaching those goals that we discussed.

I'm sure that many of the changes in Paul's life were difficult—his conversion to Christ certainly was. But they helped make Paul one of the greatest people who ever lived.

Change must happen if we are going to mature and reach our goals in life.

The Four D's

Write four new timelines on the board and label them "Physical," "Social," "Mental," and "Spiritual."

Say: **There are many changes in each of these areas that are part of the growing-up process. And these changes can lead to some wonderful privileges and benefits. Let's look at one benefit for each of these areas.** Write the following benefits on the board near the right ends of the lines. Use the brief explanation of each benefit as needed.

Physical—DO

This word indicates "freedom," being able to do things for yourself.

Social—DEEPEN

This word indicates active, growing friendships.

Mental—DECIDE

As young people mature, they have the ability and are given the opportunity to make many decisions about their lives and the future.

Spiritual—DISCOVER

Older, mature individuals are able to discover many wonderful truths about God and His Word, and move into a deeper relationship with Christ.

After writing the benefits on the lines and explaining them briefly, discuss with your group members what the process might be for each timeline. Here are some possible answers.

Physical

Babies and small children are limited to their cribs or playpens; everything must be done for them, including moving, changing, and feeding. As they grow older, their world expands. The next step is the house, and then the neighborhood, and then the school. And at each growth stage, they can do more on their own. When they become adults, they are able to do things for themselves, almost anywhere they want.

Social

Babies and small children are not really concerned with friendship; they're too busy exploring their own world. As children mature, they seek out friends to play with and, later, to "hang out" with. Older teens and adults look for friendships that involve mutual support and accountability.

Mental

For most of the early years, kids think only in terms of facts. Then they move into the world of ideas and concepts. Eventually they learn to see the "big picture" and to gather the right information for making intelligent decisions.

Spiritual

Very young children learn Bible *stories*. Those a little older learn Bible *facts*. Eventually, they learn Bible *truths* and *concepts* and how to apply them to their lives.

If you have time, instruct group members to turn Student Sheet 2-B over and create a couple new timelines. Along each line, have them write some of the changes that they are experiencing. Then have them write the goal that those changes are leading to.

5 Wrapping It Up

Summarize the session by saying something like: **You are changing in all areas of life: physical, social, mental, and spiritual. Although these changes can be frustrating and difficult, inevitably they lead to many benefits and increased privileges: "Do," "Deepen," "Decide," and "Discover," to name a few.**

Perhaps the most exciting change is in your relationship with God. As you mature, you can know Him on a deeper level, understanding His Word, seeing what He wants you to do, and having a close relationship with Him.

Close by leading group members in a time of prayer in which they thank God for the changes that He is causing in each area of their lives.

Options for Use in Youth Group

Big Wheel Speedway

If you have the room, begin the meeting with a Big Wheel (or tricycle) race. Divide into teams and give each team a Big Wheel (or tricycle) to ride around a prescribed course. When one person ends, the next one begins. The team to finish first, wins.

Bottle Races

Have a contest among volunteers or team representatives to see who can be the first to drink a baby bottle full of a soft drink. Have volunteers pair up. Give one person in each pair a "diaper" to wear (a towel with safety pins), and have that person sit on the lap of his or her partner, who will "feed" him or her the bottle.

Adapting the Session for Sixth Graders

For "Rhythm Band," don't distribute balloons (the temptation to pop them will be too great). Also, you may not want to use Student Sheet 2-B because it's a bit too conceptual for sixth graders. Instead, tell them about Paul and how he changed. Then go to the board, draw the timelines, and discuss "The Four D's."

As a Child

2-A

"When I was a child, I talked like a child, I thought like a child, I reasoned like a child. When I became a man, I put childish ways behind me" (I Corinthians 13:11).

Draw a picture or symbol of what this verse means.

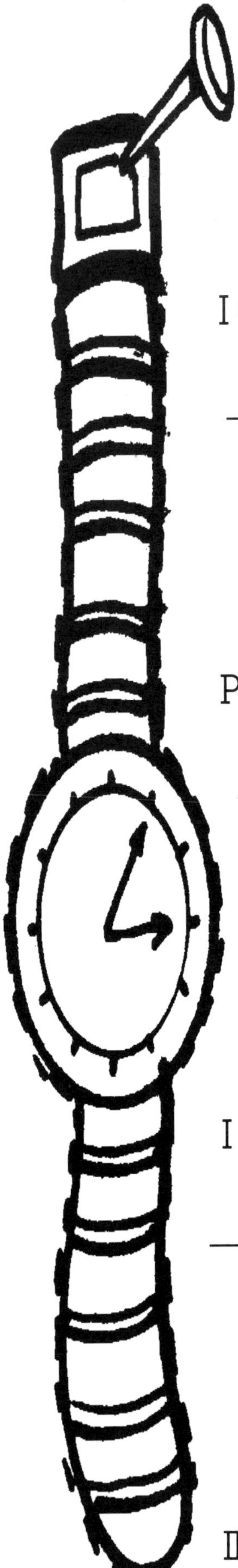

Timelines

I Corinthians 9:24-27

Philippians 3:12-14

I Timothy 4:7-10

II Timothy 4:7, 8

Session 3

Junior high can be pretty frustrating for kids because of the changes—or lack of changes—in their lives. Most of the boys in this age group, for example, are small and wish they were bigger. They see themselves as football stars; but by eighth grade, many of them still look like they're in grade school. Have you ever called the home of one of the guys in your group and mistaken his voice for his mother's? It's an easy mistake to make.

Or consider the girls. Because they usually develop sooner, many of them tower over boys their age. Some junior high girls could pass for high schoolers or older. And with their growing interest in the opposite sex, having so many "little" boys around can be maddening.

Then think of how kids feel when they see that some of their classmates have begun to grow while they remain "little" (or vice versa). Our kids need to know that they are not strange because they are "over-" or "underdeveloped." Everyone grows at a different rate, following God's perfect timing.

In Your Own Time

[Affirming That Different People Grow Up in Different Ways]

What You Want to Do

- Help kids understand that God created in each person a unique timetable for physical maturation;
- Help kids understand that people who mature early or late are not "strange," but are merely following God's timetable for them.

Where You'll Find Help

- Psalm 75:2
- Ecclesiastes 3:1
- Luke 3:23
- Romans 5:6
- II Peter 3:8, 9

What You'll Need

- Bibles
- Pencils
- Copies of "Time for a Change" (Student Sheet 3-A)
- Copies of "Ex-spurts" (Student Sheet 3-B)
- Two tables
- Building blocks
- A watch

1 Time to Build

Divide into two teams and have each team sit in parallel columns, facing the front. Put a table in front of each team. On each table place a bag of assorted building blocks. Explain that the goal is to see which team can build the highest tower of blocks in three minutes. However, this is a relay, so each person must run to the table, place one block on the team's tower and then return to his or her seat. Then the next person does the same thing, and so on, until the time is up.

2 Good Timing

Get everyone seated. Instruct kids to be quiet and to close their eyes. Explain that they should keep their eyes closed while you time one minute on your watch. They should stand when they think a minute has elapsed.

After about 70 seconds or so, have group members open their eyes. Explain that a minute was up about ten seconds ago. Comment on how soon and how late some of them stood and who stood the closest to the correct time.

Point out to your group members that this session is about timing. You're going to be talking about why different people mature at different times.

3 God's Timing

Distribute copies of "Time for a Change" (Student Sheet 3-A). Have your group members form pairs. Instruct the pairs to first complete the picture by following the dots. Then have them look up each passage and summarize its meaning.

Ask: **What did all the verses have in common?** ("Time" or "timing.")

Then look at the passages, one at a time. Read the verses aloud and have each pair share what it wrote as the meaning. Summarize answers with the following phrases, and write them on the board.

Psalm 75:2—God chooses the right time.

Ecclesiastes 3:1—There is a time for everything.

Luke 3:23—Jesus waited until He was 30 to begin His public ministry.

Romans 5:6—God does things "at just the right time."

II Peter 3:8, 9—Time never limits God.

4 Cases

Say something like: **We've been talking about growing up and about changes. Your body is changing a lot, and that can be frustrating, especially when you see others who look the way you want to look. But it's important to remember two words: God's timing. In other words, you will grow the way God wants you to grow, at just the right time. Of course that's easy for me to say, but listen to what these kids did.**

Read the following case studies aloud.

Karen has always been tall for her age, but she really noticed her height last year in seventh grade. She was taller than most of her girlfriends and at least a head taller than any of the boys she knew. She felt like a freak, a giant. But one day Karen was talking to a woman at church. This woman was very attractive and had a wonderful husband and great kids. As they were talking, the woman shared how she had been the tallest person in her whole junior high, and how the other girls and boys caught up to her in high school. She also explained the advantages of being tall. Karen decided to try to accept her height and to be patient.

Todd has been playing football for as long as he can remember. And until this year, eighth grade, he had always been first-string. But over the summer, many of Todd's friends had begun to grow while he still stayed the same. And suddenly Todd realized that he was one of the smaller boys on the team. So he did everything possible to grow, eating the right foods, exercising, and praying every night about it. Nothing seemed to work. Sensing what Todd was feeling, Todd's dad decided to have a talk with him. His dad explained how kids grow at different rates and how many boys have a "growth spurt." He said that Todd would probably turn out to be his height—6' 2". He urged Todd to be patient and to trust God's timing. Although Todd didn't feel wonderful right away, he did think about what his dad had said and decided to try thanking God for how He had made him.

Add your own case study, sharing what you were like in junior high and when you had your "growth spurt."

5 Putting It All Together

Briefly review the main points of the session, pointing out the following to your group members:

- God wants the very best for them, and His timing is perfect. The Bible makes this clear in several passages (in the Old *and* New Testaments).
- Just because a person is "too big" or "too small" for his or her age doesn't

mean the person is weird.

- Every person is unique, with his or her own special "growth timetable."
- Each person should be patient with God's timetable and not gauge his or her self-worth by the timetables of others.

Close with a time of silent prayer, urging group members to thank God for making them the way He did, with their own special timetables.

6 Ex-spurts

Distribute "Ex-spurts" (Student Sheet 3-B). Assign each group member to use his or her sheet to interview three or four adults about when their "growth spurts" occured. Instruct the group members to ask for some details about the growth spurts. Did they seem to occur too early? Too late? Did the growth spurts, or lack of them, ever cause the interviewees any embarrassment?

Tell the group members to bring these sheets with them next week so they can share what they learned.

Option for Use in Youth Group

Beat the Clock

Advertise the meeting as "Beat the Clock." Then feature a number of games where individuals have to complete a task before a certain time limit. Examples of some possible tasks include: trying to finish a child's puzzle, eating a bag of chips, blowing up and breaking a balloon, drinking a Coke, etc.

Afterward, point out that sometimes we wish we could "beat the clock" when it comes to maturing. We wish we could speed up (or slow down) God's timetable for our development.

Adapting the Session for Sixth Graders

For the "God's Timing" section, you may want to avoid having kids form pairs and filling out the worksheets on their own. Instead, discuss the worksheets together as a group.

Time *for a* Change . . . .

3-A

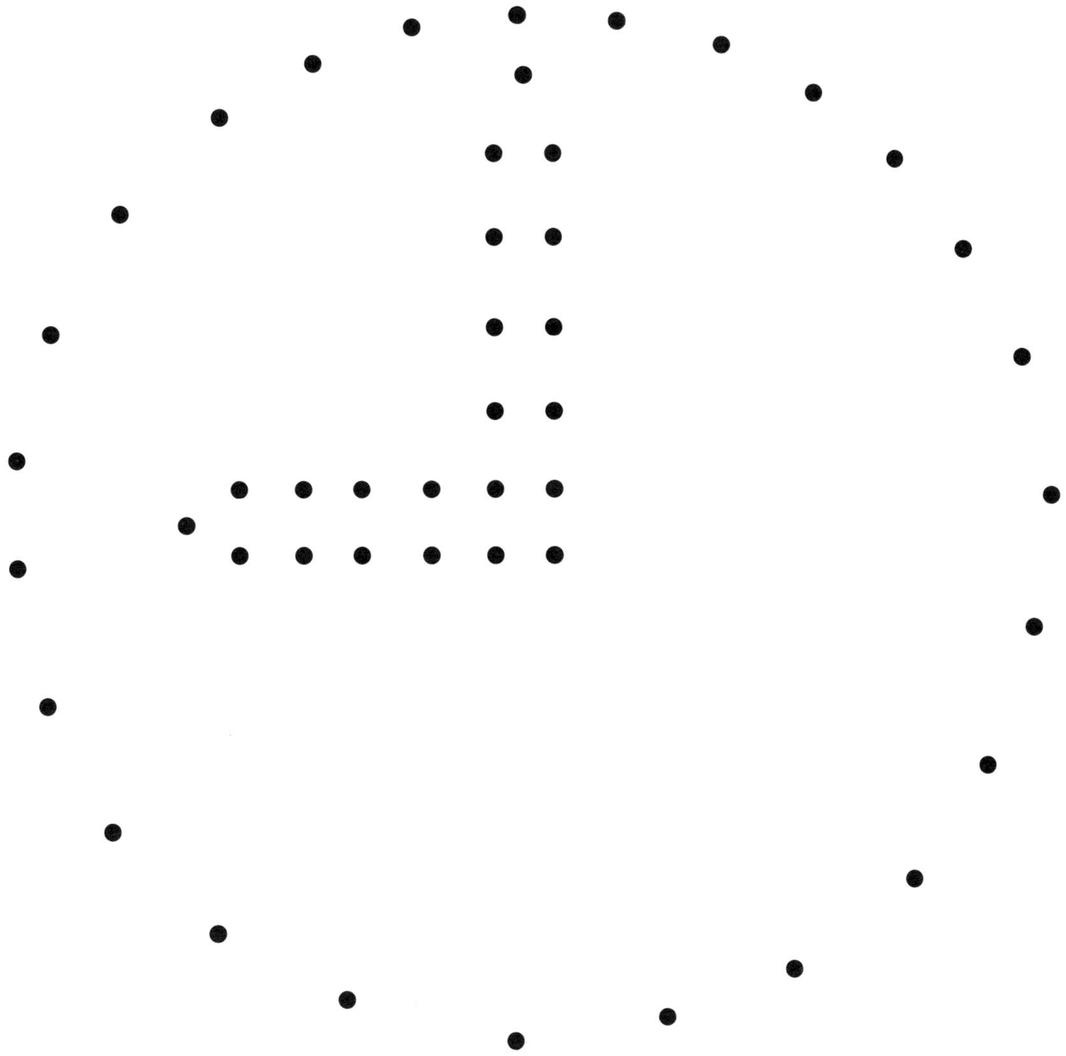

Psalm 75:2 ______________________________

Ecclesiastes 3:1 ______________________________

Luke 3:23 ______________________________

Romans 5:6 ______________________________

II Peter 3:8, 9 ______________________________

3-B

Ex-spurts

Person #1 ____________________________

Details of the growth spurt:

Person #2 ____________________________

Details of the growth spurt:

Person #3 ____________________________

Details of the growth spurt:

Person #4 ____________________________

Details of the growth spurt:

Session 4

Because junior high kids are in the middle of an enormous transition, they will often try to speed up the process, trying to act older and more mature than they really are. You can see it in their appearances (clothes, make-up, hairstyles, etc.), in the way they act, and in their choice of entertainment (PG-13 and R-rated movies and videos, etc.); and you can hear it in their language (swearing, talking gross, telling dirty stories).

This urge to be older can lead to many problems, including involvement with alcohol, drugs, sex, and gangs. When I was in junior high, I remember throwing an egg at a car to prove I was tough and to be accepted by a certain group of kids. Many junior highers do that and worse, including vandalism, shoplifting, and other antisocial acts. These young people need to know that it's all right to be their age—to be kids—and that they will have plenty of time to grow up.

No Need to Rush

[Growing Up Too Fast]

What You Want to Do

- Help kids identify potential problems created by trying to speed up God's timetable;
- Help kids understand that they can enjoy their present stage in life.

Where You'll Find Help

- Genesis 29:20-28
- Psalm 40:1-4
- Isaiah 40:31
- Romans 8:24, 25
- James 1:2-4

What You'll Need

- Bibles
- Copies of "Cut It Out!" (Student Sheet 4-A)
- Copies of "A Timely Puzzle" (Student Sheet 4-B)
- Pencils
- Envelope and slips of paper with situations on them for "Slow Motion"
- Scissors
- Tape
- Magazine pictures
- Houseplant
- Record or audiotape and record or audiotape player (with variable speeds)
- Poster board and pens

1 Ex-spurts Revisited (optional)

If you used Session 3, have the group members who did the "Ex-spurts" (Student Sheet 3-B) assignment from last week share their most interesting interviews. Discuss their interviews briefly.

2 Slow Motion

This can be done individually or in teams, depending on the size of your group. Before the session, write the following situations on separate slips of paper and place them in an envelope:

- being knocked out in a boxing match;
- telling a very funny joke to a friend;
- learning that you failed a test;
- hitting a home run to win the game;
- licking an ice-cream cone and having the ice cream drop out;
- trying to stay awake in a boring class;
- seeing a beautiful girl (handsome guy) and then walking into a tree because you're not watching where you're going.

Have each individual or team draw a slip of paper from the envelope and act out the situation *in slow motion* so that the rest of the group can guess what is happening. Tell participants to make their presentations creative, funny, and realistic.

After giving them a minute to prepare, have the individuals or teams act out their slow motion situations.

(You'll use this activity as an illustration later in the session.)

3 Cut It Out!

Distribute "Cut It Out!" (Student Sheet 4-A). Instruct group members to fold their papers "accordion" style. Distribute scissors and tell everyone to create his or her own design by cutting the folded paper on both sides.

For this to work, there must be two or three places along the fold that are uncut. You may want to demonstrate this first so that your group members will know what to do. Afterward, pick up all the scrap paper and collect the scissors. Then have group members display their designs and tape them to the board.

Say something like: **Your designs remind me of snowflakes. Do you know what is said about snowflakes? No two are alike. Each one is beautiful and unique. And that's true about people—created by God, no two are alike. Each person is beautiful and unique. The problem is that sometimes we don't like the way we are, so we try to be different. Or like our first activity, it may seem as though our lives are in slow motion, so we try to hurry the process of growing up. But God loves us as we are, and He has a perfect timetable for the changes in our lives. Let's take a closer look at the problem of trying to act older.**

Before the meeting, cut some pictures out of a magazine like *Seventeen*. These pictures should be of high school kids. Try to get the following: a beautiful, well-developed girl; a handsome, muscular boy; a tough-looking boy or girl; a popular music star.

Hold up the pictures one at a time. Say something like: **Here's someone who's older. Maybe most of you girls (guys) would like to look like her (him).**

What do some junior high girls (guys) do to try to be like this girl (guy)?

Possible answers:

For the beautiful girl—wear make-up, dress sexy, color their hair, etc.

For the handsome boy—show off muscles, wear certain clothes, etc.

For the tough-looking boy or girl—wear certain clothes, act tough, swear, smoke, make fun of kids, etc.

For the popular music star—dress like him or her, etc.

Then ask: **What are some other ways kids try to act older than they are?** Briefly discuss things like drinking, taking drugs, shoplifting, swearing, joining gangs, talking back to parents and teachers, etc.

Then say: **Usually we can see when someone else is being phony and trying to act older. But sometimes we act that way, too—especially when we're impatient and want to grow up in a hurry. Instead of trying to be something we're not, we should relax and enjoy the way we are.**

4 What's Wrong with This?

Bring out a small plant in a pot and hold it up so that everyone can see it. Then, pretend to pull on the plant, saying something like: **Come on! Grow! Hurry up! Get bigger!**

Then ask: **What's wrong with what I just did?**

After a few answers, explain: **The point is that growth takes time and can't be hurried. In fact, it takes hundreds of years to grow a giant redwood tree. There's no way to hurry up that slow and steady growth.**

Bring out a record or a tape and explain to your group members that you want to play a song for them. Then play the song at a faster speed than it was intended to be played at.

Ask: **What's wrong with this?** (The song must be played at the right speed or it will sound weird and be distorted.)

Tape a piece of poster board to the wall. Bring out a handful of felt-tipped pens and explain to your group members that you are going to draw a masterpiece for them. Then draw something on the poster board as fast as you can.

Ask: **What's wrong with this?** (A great work of art takes time to create.)

Explain that other things also take time and should not be rushed—like the birth of a baby or the development of a friendship.

Say something like: ***You* are like a solid, giant redwood tree. It will take time for you to grow and mature into the kind of creation that God wants. *You* are like a magnificent symphony, and you must be played at the right speed, as the composer and arranger intended. Being played too fast will distort the sound. *You* are like the artistic masterpiece, being drawn by the master artist. It takes time for Him to draw you just right.**

5 A Timely Puzzle

Distribute "A Timely Puzzle" (Student Sheet 4-B). Make sure that everyone has access to an NIV Bible. Explain that the answers to the puzzle are found in the verses at the bottom of the sheet. Instruct group members to look up the verses and then find the key word that fits the spaces in the puzzle.

After a few minutes, check their answers. The answers are Isaiah 40:31—HOPE; Genesis 29:20-28—YEARS; Psalm 40:1-4—TRUST; James 1:2-4—PERSEVERANCE; Romans 8:24, 25—WAIT.

Divide into five groups. Give each group one of the passages to look at again. Have the groups determine how the passages relate to the topic of "growing up too fast." They should be prepared to share their findings with the whole group.

After the groups report, summarize their answers with the following:

Isaiah 40:31—Your *hope* is in the Lord. Sometimes you may feel like giving up because you're not growing up quickly enough or because you don't look like you'd like to look. God knows what you're going through and has the solution. Hope in Him.

Genesis 29:20-28—Eventually Jacob worked 14 years before he was able to marry Rachel. That's patience and perseverance. But it was worth the wait because Jacob loved Rachel. Patience pays off.

Psalm 40:1-4—Although David was going through some tough times, he "waited patiently for the Lord." David could do this because he had trust in God, knowing that God wanted only the very best for him.

James 1:2-4—A sign of maturity is perseverance, the ability to stick with a job and get it done. You can learn perseverance by being patient and working through your problems. People who run from their problems or who try to avoid anything that is difficult don't get the chance to grow.

Romans 8:24, 25—Here are those key words again: "hope," "patiently," and "wait." Sometimes there's nothing you can do about a situation (like how tall you are)—all you can do is wait.

6 Pair Prayer

Close the session by reminding group members of what you've covered: growing up isn't something to fear, and God will be with us in the process; there are many benefits and privileges associated with growing older, one of which is being able to relate to God on a deeper level; God has created a personal timetable for growth in each person, so we shouldn't be worried or upset if we grow faster or slower than others; sometimes it's tempting to want to grow up faster, but we should appreciate and enjoy our present stage of development.

Have group members form pairs and pray for each other, that they will patiently await God's timing for growth in their lives.

Option for Use in Youth Group

Polaroid Scavenger Hunt

To illustrate the desire of many young people to see *immediate* results in the growing-up process, have a Polaroid Scavenger Hunt. Divide the group into two teams, and give each team an instant (self-developing) camera. Then give the teams a list of places and things in your local area to take pictures of. Set a time limit. The team with the most pictures of the places and things on the list, wins. Instruct your group members to be careful.

Your list can be as creative and "wacky" as you'd like. You may ask them for a picture of five people crammmed into a phone booth. Or you may ask them for a picture of the inside of the cab of a garbage truck. Or you may ask them for a picture of a local shop owner. The choice is yours.

Adapting the Session for Sixth Graders

Don't do "Slow Motion" with everyone in the group. Instead, select outgoing and confident individuals to perform for the rest of the group. Do "A Timely Puzzle" as individuals, and don't break into groups to discuss the verses. Instead, have someone read a passage aloud; then discuss it as a group. Pray together instead of breaking into pairs for prayer at the end.

Cut It Out!

4-A

4-B

A Timely Puzzle

1. Isaiah 40:31

2. Genesis 29:20-28

3. Psalm 40:1-4

4. James 1:2-4

5. Romans 8:24, 25

Session 5

In a recent survey of teenagers (ages 13-18), 68% of those polled considered themselves to be adults. As a result, many of them felt they deserved more independence than they currently enjoyed. Most parents, on the other hand, do not consider their teens to be adults; they feel teens enjoy enough independence—maybe too much.

The problem is that teens—junior highers, in particular—are more dependent on parents than they realize, and parents know this. Most parents know their young teens depend on them for food, shelter, clothing, transportation, instruction, and much more.

Junior highers feel they do not have enough independence; parents feel they do. Put these two perceptions together, mix in the extra truth that in a few short years the young teen should be equipped to function independently of mom and dad and you have a potentially stressful situation.

The Long Road to Independence

[Parents]

What You Want to Do

- Help kids understand that their growing desire for independence may be in conflict with their parents' continued desire for control;
- Help kids empathize with their parents' struggle to "let go";
- Help kids brainstorm ways they can work with their parents to ease the anxiety of independence.

Where You'll Find Help

- Ephesians 6:1-3

What You'll Need

- Bibles
- Pencils
- Copies of "Parenthood" (Student Sheet 5-A)
- Copies of "The Independence Meter" (Student Sheet 5-B)
- Paper

1 If I Were a Parent

Distribute copies of "Parenthood" (Student Sheet 5-A). Have your group members fill out the first section. Allow about two minutes for them to fill it out. Then go quickly through each statement and encourage volunteers to share their parental ideals.

Ask: **What is the toughest thing about being a parent?**

How do parents learn to be parents? (Trial and error; from how their parents raised them; from watching what others do, etc.)

Say something like: **There are many different ideas about how parenting should be done. Many parents wonder if they're doing it right—after all, there's no such thing as a parenting school that teaches a person the specifics of raising a child.**

Today we're going to learn how you can make your parents' job easier—and how *you* can begin to enjoy more independence—by following what the Bible says.

2 A Look at God's Word

Have group members turn to Ephesians 6:1-3 in their Bibles. Ask a volunteer to read aloud the passage. Draw the group's attention to verse 1.

Ask: **What do you think this verse means when it says to "obey your parents in the Lord"?** (Responses may include: "Obey Mom and Dad like God would want me to"; "Obey Mom and Dad unless they asked me to do something ungodly"; "Go to church when they say to"; "Do what they say to do.")

Now look at verse 2 together.

Ask: **How do we "honor" our parents? What are some ways we can do this?** (Obey them; show affection to them; respect them; take out the garbage when they ask; treat them well, etc.)

After the kids offer their responses, point out that to "honor" their parents can mean:

1. to prize them highly (treat them like a treasure);
2. to care for them (to be concerned about how they feel, to show love to them);
3. to show respect for them (give them special treatment, recognize their authority, compliment them on their good ideas);
4. to obey them (do chores the first time they ask, etc.).

3 A Story of Action

Say: **I'm going to read a little story. As I read the story, certain people in the group will stand and perform an action when I call out key words.**

If you can assign the actions secretly to each group, it will be more fun. Give the following instructions to the appropriate people.

- All guys with a last name that begins with a letter between A and L should stand and pantomime polishing a trophy when you say the word "prize" or any form of the word ("prized," "prizing," etc.).
- All girls with a last name that begins with a letter between A and L should stand and salute every time you say the word "respect" or any form of the word ("respected," "respecting," etc.).
- All guys with a last name that begins with a letter between M and Z should stand and pantomime rocking a baby in their arms every time you say the word "care" or any form of the word ("cared," "caring," etc.).
- All girls with a last name that begins with a letter between M and Z should stand and shout "Yes, sir!" or "Yes, ma'am!" every time you say the word "obey" or any form of the word ("obeyed," "obeying," etc.)

Make sure the kids understand their assignments; then begin the story.

4 The Story of Mark

Once there was a guy named Mark. He was a pretty independent guy who didn't honor his parents. He didn't *obey* them, he didn't show he *cared* for them, and he didn't show *respect* for them. He acted like he didn't need them, and he certainly didn't *prize* them. His relationship to his parents was basically the pits.

As Mark grew older, he showed even less *care* and *respect* to his parents. He never *obeyed* them anymore, and he never *prized* them. As a result of this Mark didn't *prize, obey, respect,* or *care* for any adult.

When Mark was in high school, he had many jobs. But he would always lose them because he didn't *prize* his work, he didn't *respect* his customers, he didn't *care* about the people he worked with, and he didn't *obey* his boss.

Finally Mark had to take a look at his life, because he was sad. He had no relationship with his parents, he disliked all his teachers, and he couldn't even hold a job. He began to realize that other people were treating him like he treated them. Nobody seemed to *prize, respect,* or *care* for him. And certainly no one *obeyed* him.

After thinking it over, he said to himself, "If I don't honor others by *prizing, caring* for, *respecting,* and *obeying* them, I'm just hurting myself."

Mark made a complete change. He determined to honor his parents and other authorities. "I'll *prize, care* for, *respect*, and *obey* my parents and *obey, prize, care* for, and *respect* my teachers and employers from now on," he declared. And Mark lived happily ever after.

Look at Ephesians 6:3 together.

Say: **The Bible says honor your parents so that it "may go well with you and that you may enjoy long life on the earth."**

What kind of life did Mark have when he didn't honor his parents? (He was lonely, frustrated, irresponsible, etc.)

What kind of improvements in his life can he expect due to his attitude change? (He will have a happier home life; he should be able to keep a job; he will have better working relationships; he might make better grades; other people will begin to treat him better, etc.)

In what ways could you expect your life to "go well" and "be long" if you honor your parents? (Answers should be similar to the answers to the previous question.)

Do you think your parents would be willing to allow you more independence if you showed them that you were trying to honor them? Why or why not? Allow time for volunteers to respond.

5 Feeling Like a Parent

Say: **Let's take a few minutes to see what it might feel like to be the parent of a teenager.**

Have the kids fill out the bottom section of Student Sheet 5-A.

Ask: **Of all the situations described in this exercise, which would be toughest for you to deal with if you were a parent? Why?**

Now that you have an idea of how your parents may sometimes feel, think of how honoring them, as the Bible teaches, would make their lives easier. (It would lessen their stress; they would feel better about allowing me more independence, etc.)

6 Independence Meter

Say: **Let's take a look at how much independence you already have.** Hand out copies of "The Independence Meter" (Student Sheet 5-B). Allow the kids time to complete the worksheet.

In discussing the sheets, try to avoid having kids compare results. You don't want to make people feel worse than they already do about their level of independence.

Say something like: **Many of you probably have achieved *some* inde-**

pendence already. How does it feel to realize that? Does it seem like you're independent? Allow time for response.

Then go through the 15 items on the "Independence Meter." For each item, ask: **What are some of the responsibilities that go with this freedom?** (Example: If a teen is able to go to the mall, there are probably certain rules that he or she must abide by, such as: "Don't leave the mall for any reason until mom or dad picks you up" or "Be where I am going to pick you up *on time*." These are responsibilities that accompany the independent act of going to the mall alone.)

As the kids discuss the responsibilities attached to the "acts of independence," stress the fact that *responsibility earns independence*. If a kid demonstrates reliability in his or her responsibilities, he or she will receive more independence.

Say: **If you're demanding freedom and independence from mom and dad, yet not earning it by being responsible in other areas—making your bed, cleaning your room, doing your homework, etc.—you're going to cause a lot of tension between your parents and yourself. You're not honoring your parents when you do this, and their response is usually to tighten the grip on your life rather than loosen it.**

On the other hand, if you show responsibility over a long period of time, your parents will probably give you independence more quickly. You will be rewarded for honoring your parents. Life will go well with you, and you'll live long in the land.

7 Making Mom and Dad's Job Easier

Have kids form the same groups they were in for the "Story of Mark" exercise. Instruct the groups to brainstorm some ways they can work with their parents to ease their parents' anxiety about independence.

Give the groups some of the following examples to get them started:

- Don't say things that will hurt your parents' feelings like, "I can't wait until I'm old enough to move out of here."
- Don't cop out on your responsibilities—keep your room clean, mow the lawn without complaint, etc.
- Write your parents a note expressing your thankfulness for them.
- Thank God for your parents.
- Remember that parents are people, too.
- Don't allow yourself to talk down about your parents to anyone.
- Exercise good judgment in choosing your own clothes and hairstyle, in spending your money, and in any other responsibilities you are currently allowed.

After a few minutes, have the groups share their ideas.

Close the session in prayer, asking God for His help as your kids struggle with and for their independence.

Options for Use in Youth Group

"Just Like Mom and Dad" Dress-Up Contest

Divide into teams, with boys and girls on separate teams. Each team should have a complete outfit of "mom" or "dad" clothes. (Boys get dad's clothes; girls get mom's clothes.)

When you say "Go," the first person in each team puts on (over his or her own clothes) the "mom" or "dad" outfit and then takes it off as quickly as possible. Then the next member of the team does the same thing. The first team to have all its group members put on and take off the outfit is the winner.

"Reminders of Mom and Dad" Scavenger Hunt

Divide (perhaps by birthday months) into teams. Each team needs a pencil, paper, and a secretary. Instruct each team to work together to find 20 items (from wallets, purses, clothing, etc.) that reminds the team members of their parents. This could be a shirt bought by a team member's mother, a picture of a team member's grandfather, etc. The first team to find and list 20 items wins. Have the winning team read its list and explain why the items remind team members of their parents.

Adapting the Session for Sixth Graders

Gauge your sixth graders carefully to determine whether they will understand the "If I Were a Parent" exercise. You may need to drop it. You may also want to eliminate the "Feeling Like a Parent" exercise.

On the other hand, the dress-up contest from the "Options for Use in Youth Group" section would work well with sixth graders. You may want to consider using it as an opener.

Parenthood

5-A

Congratulations! You are the parent of a teenager! Pretty exciting idea, huh?! Well, try your hand at being a parent by filling in the spaces below with as many good ideas as you can come up with in two minutes.

If I Were the Parent of a Teenager . . .

. . . I would never . . .
(yell at my kid)

. . . I would always . . .
(respect his/her privacy)

. . . I would try. . .
(to understand him/her)

. . . I would be . . .
(really nice to him/her)

. . . I'd help my teen by . . .
(taking time to talk)

. . . I'd encourage my teen by . . .
(noticing when he/she does good things, not just bad things)

Feeling Like a Parent . . .

I would feel . . .

______________ when the teen who once loved to be around me now sometimes seems embarrassed around me.

______________ when my child becomes a teenager and doesn't hug me as often as he or she used to.

______________ when my teen doesn't talk to me as openly as he or she used to.

______________ when my child, who used to want to play with me over anyone else, would now rather be with friends than with me.

______________ when I notice how quickly my teen is growing up.

______________ when the child who was so dependent on me for everything now needs me for very little.

The Independence Meter

5-B

Put an "x" in the column that is closest to the truth in your life.

	Always	Sometimes	Rarely	Never
1. I choose my own music.				
2. I spend my money any way I want to.				
3. I choose my own hairstyle.				
4. I pick out my own clothes.				
5. I don't ask mom and dad for money.				
6. I go to the mall and to movies without my parents.				
7. I have a job (paper route, babysitting, etc.).				
8. I pick my own friends.				
9. I obey my curfew, or go home when I am supposed to.				
10. I choose my own elective classes at school.				
11. I keep my room clean, make my own bed, etc.				
12. I press, fold, and put away my own clothes.				
13. I cook some of my own meals.				
14. I do my homework without being told to.				
15. I do chores around the house after being told only once.				

Session 6

"Hey, Rich, why do you go to church? I didn't think anybody did that anymore."

This question can greatly intimidate many teenagers, especially those in middle school and junior high. It is intimidating both because young teens so want to be like everyone else and because they often find it difficult to know how to answer a question like, "Why do you go to church?" Some of them are beginning to ask themselves the same question as they begin to "own" their faith.

Additionally, sharing expressions of faith, such as going to church, can make teens feel "different" and "outside," which makes them very uncomfortable. They want other kids to agree with and accept what they say; unfortunately, this cannot be guaranteed, especially when they talk of a "personal relationship with God." So instead of risking rejection for being "different," they would rather just not share at all.

With this age group we should stress the importance of developing Christian character traits like serving and kindness (taking clothing to a shelter for the homeless, delivering meals to the homebound, etc.). Show your junior highers that they can let their deeds do the talking as they gain the ability to share their faith in other ways.

A New Responsibility to Your Friends

[Modeling Christianity]

What You Want to Do

- Help kids recognize their responsibility to demonstrate to their friends what being a Christian is all about;
- Help kids brainstorm practical, nonthreatening ways they can live their faith.

Where You'll Find Help

- Matthew 5:14-16

What You'll Need

- Bibles
- Pencils
- Copies of "The Cure for AIDS" (Student Sheet 6-A)
- Copies of "Ideas Alphabet" (Student Sheet 6-B)
- Chalkboard and chalk or newsprint and marker
- Seven sheets of paper, each with one of the following words written on it: "You," "are," "the," "light," "of," "the," "world"
- Flashlight
- Large, opaque bowl
- Blankets, tape, etc. to light-proof your meeting place

1 The Cure for AIDS

Hand out copies of "The Cure for AIDS" (Student Sheet 6-A). Have kids work individually on them. When the kids are through, get a few of their responses to both parts of the worksheet and their reasons for answering as they did.

Say something like: **In the first section of the worksheet most of you said you would share your great discovery with others, to bring many people the benefit of this cure.**

Ask: **How long can the average person in our part of the world hope to live?** (Between 70 and 80 years.)

Would you say AIDS is the one of the most deadly diseases known today? (Probably yes.)

What would you say if I told you there was an even deadlier disease than AIDS, one that could kill not only your physical body, but your soul, as well? Get a few brief reactions.

Then say: **Well, there is a worse disease. It's called sin. Because of it we could be separated from God forever unless we accept Jesus' sacrifice for our sins and give ourselves to Him by faith.**

If you knew the cure for AIDS, you would share it with people, so they could live out their 70 or 80 years of life. How much more necessary do you think it is to share the cure for sin—Jesus and His work on the cross—with your friends so they can live forever? Allow time for group members to share their opinions.

Ask: **Why is it so difficult to share about Jesus with our friends?** Encourage several group members to respond honestly. Acknowledge that sharing our faith can be very scary; but point out that it's important that we conquer our fear—for our friends' sake.

Refer back to the bottom section of Student Sheet 6-A. Instruct the kids to insert the words "good news about Jesus" for "cure" or "cured" (this may require slight rewording) in the questions. Then discuss as a group what is wrong or right with these ideas.

2 Hidden Secrets

Before the session, write each of the first seven words of Matthew 5:14 ("You," "are," "the," "light," "of," "the," "world") on an individual sheet of paper. Then fold the seven sheets and hide them around the room. Remember where you hid them. Also be sure to block off any cracks or windows in the room where light might get in.

Turn off the lights and shine a flashlight on yourself as you speak. Say: **In this room is a very important secret message that God wants you to know—but you must find it in the dark. Begin now.** Don't tell the kids any more than this about the message. Turn off the flashlight. Let them wander around for 20-30 seconds.

Say: **It's pretty difficult finding the message in the dark, isn't it? Well, let me give you a little help. I'll turn on this flashlight—but I'm going to cover it with this bowl.** Turn on the flashlight, lay it down, and cover it with an opaque bowl. Say: **Now look for the secret message.** Let the kids wander for another 20-30 seconds.

Say: **This isn't easy, is it? Let me help you.** Pick up the flashlight. **You are looking for folded pieces of paper which will have words on them. I'll point out the hiding places of these pieces of paper. Try to be the first person to find each piece and bring it to me when I point the light at it.** Point at each hiding place until someone brings the paper to you. Put the sheets on the floor in the order you receive them.

When all the papers have been gathered, have the kids put them in proper order. Then turn on the lights.

Ask: **How did you feel groping in the darkness for something you knew you needed to find?** (Frustrated.)

How did it feel to not even really know what you were looking for? (Irritating.)

Was the light helpful? (Yes, it was probably impossible to find the papers without it.)

Say: **You found the secret message—"You are the light of the world"! Let's look at Matthew 5:14-16 to get the whole idea of what the Bible means by this.**

A Group of Lights

Have someone read aloud Matthew 5:14-16.

Ask: **What does this passage describe you as?** (The light of the world and a city on a hill.)

How do you think we Christians can be lights in the world? (Someone may suggest by doing "good deeds" as stated in verse 16.)

Why would someone want to hide his or her light under a bowl? (Because the person doesn't realize what "shining his or her light" means; because the person doesn't realize how his or her light can help others.)

How would you "let your light shine before men"? One obvious way is to do good deeds, so let the kids give some specific examples of good deeds toward their parents, brothers and sisters, and others.

What would be the result of these good deeds? Point out that when we do good deeds, we are behaving as Christ would. Therefore, we will "remind" people of Christ, and the people will thank God for us and for Jesus. Encourage kids to share specific examples of this.

Say: **In the game with the flashlight, you were like your friends and people at school who aren't Christians. There is truth that God wants them to know about eternal life through His Son and the help He can give them with their problems. However, their minds are darkened because of sin, so they can't figure it out themselves.**

When I turned on the flashlight in the game, you were pointed to the secret. As Christians and lights of the world, your job is to point your friends to the *big* secret—Christ, who can bring them eternal life and answers for some of the immediate problems in their lives.

We can be lights to our friends by living our Christian lives for them to see. According to Matthew 5:14-16, we have a responsibility to be a light to everyone we know.

4 The Ideas Alphabet

Hand out copies of "The Ideas Alphabet" (Student Sheet 6-B). Have the kids form two or more groups. Instruct each group to work together to brainstorm 26 "good deeds" (acts of kindness, acts of service, good friendship tips, etc.) or ways that they can "model" Christianity to their friends—one for each letter of the alphabet. They can use the letters in words or phrases. Give them at least 10 minutes to work. (If time is short, divide up the alphabet among the groups.)

When they are finished, make a master list of the ideas on the board or on a large piece of newsprint. Compliment the kids on their ideas. You may also want to collect the lists after the session, type them up, copy them, and give them to the kids next week.

5 A Chance to Shine

Refer group members to the "Hmm, Let Me Think" section of Student Sheet 6-B. Quickly go through the situations, asking volunteers to call out ways a Christian could "shine his or her light" in each one.

Close the session in prayer, asking God for His strength as your group members attempt to be lights to their friends and other people.

Option for Use in Youth Group

Newspaper Fashion Show

Use this as an opener to the session. Divide into teams. Give each team a newspaper and six strips of tape. Explain that each team is to design a bathing suit, a dress, a hat, a shirt, or a pair of pants using the supplies you have distributed.

After several minutes, have the teams model their creations as though they are in a fashion show. You be the judge, and determine which team modeled its outfit best.

For transition into the session, say something like: **Whether you realize it or not, people can tell a lot about you just by the way you behave and by the things you do or don't do. You are modeling a certain lifestyle. Today we'll talk about how you can "model" Christianity to your friends.**

Adapting the Session for Sixth Graders

In the "Hidden Secrets" section, simplify your explanation of the activity. Comparing the flashlight to our function as Christians in the world may be too abstract for sixth graders.

Try opening the session with the "Newspaper Fashion Show." Sixth graders will be able to recognize the "modeling" connection.

The Cure for AIDS

Imagine that you had AIDS and discovered a cure for it. You tested it on yourself, you know it works, and you're now cured. Write down what you would do with the information.

How do you feel about the following responses to the above situation:

"I would keep the cure to myself."

"I would only share the cure with certain people, but not everybody."

"I would just let people see my cure and hope that it inspired them to find their own cure, whatever that might be."

Ideas Alphabet

6-B

Brainstorm 26 good deeds (ways to show kindness, ways to serve, good friendship tips, etc.) we can do to show our friends Christianity by modeling it in our lives. You may use the letters in words or phrases. Look at the following examples:

For "A" you could write: "Be **A**vailable to my friends."

For "C" you could write: "**C**are."

For "X" you could write: "Don't be obno**X**ious."

A	N
B	O
C	P
D	Q
E	R
F	S
G	T
H	U
I	V
J	W
K	X
L	Y
M	Z

Hmm, Let Me Think

Think about these situations. Ask yourself: "What would Christ do?"

- A person some people call a "geek" drops his books right in front of you.
- A kid nobody likes has a flat tire on his bike.
- Someone is gossiping about a friend of yours.
- Someone is gossiping about someone you don't like.
- A student in a wheelchair needs help finding his class quickly.
- The most popular person in school asks you to lie for him, and says you'll be a part of his group if you do.
- A person is talking against God and Christianity.
- A friend wants to know what Christianity is all about.

Session 7

In one of his comedy accounts of youth, comedian Bill Cosby laments, "At the same time that I started liking girls, God decided to change my voice and put pimples on my face." It's ironic that at the point in life when young teens are most sensitive to appearing different, they undergo such a tremendous physical change.

This is the time of the "imaginary audience," where teens get overwhelming feelings that everyone's attention is on them. So when a junior higher walks tentatively into a roomful of her peers, shielding her face with her hand, most likely she's trying to cover that zit on her forehead. She's convinced that everyone else in the room is staring at it in disgust.

The young teen beginning puberty, with all of its bodily changes and emotional readjustment, is also experiencing a time of great relational upheaval. All the young teen's key relationships (family, friends, adults, etc.) are re-evaluated. The two most obvious relational changes are the distancing from the parent and the sudden intense interest in members of the opposite sex. This is the time of the "think-about-the-person-all-the-time" crush and the first stabs at romantic love.

In this session you'll help your young teens begin to understand their newfound affection for the opposite sex and the way this affection is often experienced—as a crush. As you lead this session, be sensitive to the delicate nature of this topic.

When Crushes Replace Cooties

[The Opposite Sex]

What You Want to Do

- Help kids understand that "think-about-the-person-all-the-time" crushes are a normal part of the maturation process;
- Help kids celebrate a God wonderful enough to create romantic love.

Where You'll Find Help

- I Corinthians 13:4-8

What You'll Need

- Bibles
- Pencils
- Copies of "Love Test" (Student Sheet 7-A)
- Copies of "A Story of Romance" (Student Sheet 7-B)
- Four older teens (two girls and two guys) to serve as the "Expert Panel"
- Items for "A Story of Romance" exercise: make-up/pimple medication, a toy car, a piece of fruit, a wad of paper, a toothbrush, money, or items of your choosing

1 Word Association

Say: **Today we're going to talk about the time in life we all reach when we start thinking of members of the opposite sex as people. That's right, a time when guys actually like girls and girls like guys.**

Let's do some word association to get the those brain cells humming. I'll say different words to some of you at random (you may ask several kids the same word) **and you just say the first thing that comes to your mind, so we can see how your mind works.** Have fun with the responses.

Say to girls: **Guy.**

Say to guys: **Girl.**

Say to anyone: **Kiss. Moonlight. Crush. Love. Sweetheart. Friendship. Beautiful. Romance. Cool.**

When you finish the word association, ask: **Girls, what seemed to occupy the guys' minds?**

Guys, what seemed to occupy the girls' minds?

What do these responses show us about one another? Allow time for some brief responses.

2 Role Switch

Ask for several volunteers to come forward and participate in some humorous roleplays. Have a group of guys roleplay girls and a group of girls roleplay guys in the following situations. Assign the roleplays secretively, if possible.

Encourage your actors to use exaggeration and humor as they emphasize probable words and actions of the opposite sex.

The guys' roleplays of the girls could include:

- Picking out clothes in a clothing store with friends;
- Getting ready to go out in public (brushing hair, doing nails, etc.).

The girls' roleplays of the guys could include:

- Being tough and macho to impress girls;
- Trying to think of things to say during phone conversations with a girl.

Give guys and girls a chance to briefly defend themselves after each roleplay is done. (Girls might say: "If you guys weren't just interested in good-looking girls, we wouldn't spend so much time getting ready." Guys might say: "It's not easy to find interesting stuff to talk about on the phone. We usually don't get to talk that much around girls.") Feel free to re-route a roleplay if it starts getting out of hand.

Ask: **How did it feel to portray a member of the opposite sex?**

How did you feel after the guys/girls roleplayed you? (Perhaps angry or misunderstood.)

How many of you have a question about why guys and girls do some of the things they do? You'll probably get a lot of response, the activity having stirred your kids up.

3 Expert Panel

Say: **I know there are things about guys and girls that you are just dying to know. Today we have a panel of experts to tell you the "whys" of some of the strange behavior of the opposite sex.**

Distribute paper and pencils to group members. Have each of them write his or her "biggest question about the opposite sex" for the expert panel to answer.

Here are some suggested questions to use if necessary.

For girls:

"Why do girls seem to work harder than guys at looking attractive?"

"Why do girls like shopping more than guys do?"

"Why do girls have their friends tell guys that they like them?"

For guys:

"Why do guys feel like they need to appear tough?"

"Why do guys have their friends tell girls that they like them?"

"Why do guys sometimes avoid activities because the activities aren't 'cool'?"

"Why do guys whistle and catcall to girls—even ones they don't know?"

Collect the papers, keeping girls' and guys' questions separate. Have the members of the panel—four older teens (two guys and two girls) that you've recruited—come forward and line up their chairs in a row facing the group.

Introduce the "expert panel." Begin the discussion by asking a girl's question of the guys on the panel, then asking a guy's question of the girls on the panel. Give the panel members a chance to collaborate before they answer, but keep the pace moving. Try to avoid criticizing the panel or the questions.

When all (or most) of the questions have been answered, thank the panel members and dismiss them. Have your kids clap for the panel.

Ask: **How did it feel to know these questions were on the guys'/girls' minds?** (Probably strange or educational.)

Did you feel misunderstood? (Probably yes.)

Say: **Well, get used to it. God has made guys and girls different so we would be more interesting to each other. Which responses did you find to be most interesting?**

Love Test

Hand out copies of "Love Test" (Student Sheet 7-A). Say something like: **Even with all our misunderstandings, most of you would probably admit that you're at least a little interested in the opposite sex. As a matter of fact, you may have even experienced what's known as a "crush" on another person.**

Ask for a couple volunteers to explain what a "crush" is. If no one mentions it, suggest that a crush is what you have when you can hardly think of anything else but that "special person" in your life—who may or may not be interested in you.

Have kids fill out Part I of the worksheet.

Then get their opinions for each statement, using the following method: If they agree that the statement describes true love, have them make a kissing noise; if they feel it does not describe true love, have them stick out their tongues and do "raspberries." Discuss their reactions.

True Love Is . . .

Have kids form small groups. Instruct them to complete Part II of Student Sheet 7-A together as a group. You may want to be prepared to define words like "perseveres" for kids. When everyone has finished the sheet, discuss it, using the following questions.

Ask: **How many kids that you know have had a "think-about-the-person-all-the-time" crush?** After everyone has responded, refer to the worksheet.

Which one of these qualities do you feel is most important in a relationship? Why?

If you were thinking about starting a relationship with someone, which two of these qualities would you look for first? Why?

Which one of these qualities do you most need to develop?

Discuss their responses briefly.

Then ask: **If you were to tell your parents or other adults about a "crush" that you have on someone, how do you think they would respond?** Be prepared for quite a bit of response here.

How do you feel when people use phrases like "puppy love" to describe your relationships?

Do you ever feel like nobody understands your feelings but you? Allow time for several kids to respond. Let them vent their frustrations, but don't allow this to turn into a gripe session about parents and other adults.

Say something like: **When your parents were your age, they probably experienced the exact kinds of feelings you're experiencing right now. They**

probably know what you're going through. And when they use words like "puppy love," they may not be making fun of you. They know that at this time of your life, the feelings you're having are common.

Crushes are normal. But God has designed you so that your "love" relationships will change as you get older and begin to experience more mature feelings.

Isn't God good? Aren't you glad He understands where you are and who you will become?

6 A Story of Romance

Distribute copies of "A Story of Romance" (Student Sheet 7-B). Have kids form small groups and work on the sheet in their groups. Instruct each team to appoint a "scribe" to write down the story and a "reader" to present it.

Assign the first "story start" to half of the groups and the second "story start" to the other half. Produce the six objects (a piece of fruit, a toy car, money, make-up/pimple medicine, a wad of paper, a toothbrush, or any number of other items you feel would make great story material) and display them where all the teens can see. If you don't have the objects, list or draw them on the board.

When the groups have finished their romantic stories, have each group's "reader" read its masterpiece. When all the stories have been read, congratulate the groups on their work.

Close the session in prayer, asking God to work in your kids' early male-female relationships to help them grow and develop mature love in His timing.

Options for Use in Youth Group

If You Love Me, Honey, Smile

This is an old game, but it is a great set-up for this session's topic. Have everyone sit in a circle. Choose a person to begin. He or she must go to any person of the opposite sex, kneel down, and say, "If you love me, Honey, smile." That person then must respond, "I love you, Honey, but I just can't smile," keeping a totally straight face.

If the person who was approached doesn't smile, the first person must repeat the process with someone else. But if the person who was approached *does* smile (even slightly), he or she becomes "it" and must try to get someone else to smile.

Eskimo Kiss Lipstick Pass

Another "oldie, but goodie." Divide the group into two teams. Each team lines up, alternating by sex. Smear lipstick on the nose of the first person in each team's line. The winning team is the one that passes the lipstick smear farthest down the line in 30 seconds by "Eskimo kissing" (nose rubbing).

Adapting the Session for Sixth Graders

For sixth graders, don't do the "Role Switch" exercise. You may also want to consider dropping the opening "Word Association" exercise. Instead, use one or both of the activities in the "Options for Use in Youth Group" section. On Student Sheet 7-A, define carefully the difficult words like "perseveres." If you're short of time, leave out the activity on Student Sheet 7-B.

Love Test

Part I

Answer "Yes," "No," or "Maybe" beside each of the following statements. Be honest.

You know it's true love when:

_____ 1. You talk with the person on the phone 5-10 times a day, and sometimes you don't even say anything.

_____ 2. The person drinks out of the same cup as you—without wiping it off first.

_____ 3. The person likes everything about you—even your "puppy eyes" or your "button nose."

_____ 4. You "go together" for more than two weeks straight.

_____ 5. You hang around with each other more than with anyone else—even your best friends.

_____ 6. You think about the other person all the time.

_____ 7. The other person creates a "pet" name for you like "Boopsie" or "Punkin' Head."

_____ 8. You kiss a couple of times.

_____ 9. You hold hands and don't even worry how cold, sweaty, and clammy the other person's hands are.

_____ 10. You can pick your nose or burp in front of one another.

Part II

Translate what the Bible says about true love into your own language and experience. This exercise is based on I Corinthians 13: 4-8.

What the Bible says:	**What it means for teens with the opposite sex:**
Love is patient.	(Doesn't push me into things I don't want to do.)
Love is kind.	_______________
Love is not envious.	_______________
Love is not boastful.	_______________
Love is not proud.	_______________
Love is not rude.	_______________
Love is not self-seeking.	_______________
Love is not easily angered.	_______________
Love doesn't record wrongs.	_______________
Love doesn't delight in evil.	_______________
Love rejoices with the truth.	_______________
Love always protects.	_______________
Love always trusts.	_______________
Love always hopes.	_______________
Love always perseveres.	_______________
Love never fails.	_______________

A Story of Romance

Create a romantic tale that will be from 1-3 minutes in length. Include as many things that you've learned from today's session as possible. Begin the story with the "story start" you were assigned. Be sure to use all the objects your leader has displayed in your story. Write on the back of the sheet if you run out of room on the front.

Story Start #1

Once there was a girl named ________________ who was greatly in love with a guy named ________________. It was a moonlit night when . . .

Story Start #2

______________ (guy's name) was interested in ____________ (girl's name). He wanted to see if he could get something started so he . . .

Session 8

Many junior high teens can relate to comedian Rodney Dangerfield's lament, "I don't get no respect." One of the loudest cries of young teens is, "Notice how grown up I am and respect me!" After all, they feel grown up!

These young teens are desperately trying to detach themselves from being perceived as children. This is obvious in the way they dress, the way they wear their hair and make-up, and by their first hesitant steps into adult-style relationships.

Statistics show that junior high kids today enjoy much more freedom and less parental supervision than kids of any previous generation. They also seem to carry more responsibilities. This is largely due to the dramatic rise in two-income households where both mom and dad work, and the equally dramatic rise in single-parent homes. Teens in either of these situations must often take responsibility for the care of the household. They have an unprecedented amount of personal control over their lives.

A Little More Respect

[Understanding Society's Changing View of You]

What You Want to Do

- Help kids give voice to their feelings of being treated like "little kids" by society;
- Help kids understand how the biblical concept of "putting away childish things" can contribute to their being treated more like adults;
- Help kids brainstorm specific ways they can begin to change society's opinion of them.

Where You'll Find Help

- Luke 2:52
- I Corinthians 13:11
- I Timothy 4:12

What You'll Need

- Bibles
- Pencils
- Copies of "When I Was a Child/When I Become an Adult" (Student Sheet 8-A)
- Copies of "The Carpenter's Son" (Student Sheet 8-B)
- Group members' childhood objects
- Play-Doh

1 Childhood Memory Exercise

If possible, call your group members a few days before the meeting and tell them to bring to the meeting one object from their childhood. It may be a toy, photo, book, memento—whatever they want.

To begin the session, ask volunteers to show their objects from childhood and tell a little bit about them and why the objects are/were special to them. Ask volunteers who forgot to bring their objects to describe them and share about them from memory.

Then ask: **What is your favorite childhood memory?** If group members are reluctant to talk, share your favorite childhood memory.

How does it feel to go back into childhood? Allow time for a few kids to respond.

Do you feel like you're still being treated like a child? When? Allow time for several kids to respond.

Say something like: **As you grow older, you can expect society's view of you to change. You will begin to command more and more respect. It must be tough at times to still feel as if you're being treated like a little kid.**

2 As a Child/As an Adult

Hand out copies of "When I Was a Child/When I Become an Adult" (Student Sheet 8-A). Say: **I Corinthians 13:11 says, "When I was a child, I talked like a child, I thought like a child, I reasoned like a child. When I became a man, I put childish ways behind me." Fill out this worksheet and we'll see what childish things you've left behind you and what adult things you'll be picking up in the next ten years.**

Have the kids complete the worksheet according to the instructions. Give them 5-10 minutes to do this. When everyone is finished, go quickly through the sheet and have volunteers call out their answers.

Ask: **How many things in your life will change from five years ago to ten years from now?** (Almost everything.)

What was the best thing to you about being a kid? (Responses might include: "I was able to play around a lot.")

What will be the best thing about being an adult? (Responses might include: "You get to do what you want when you want.")

What are some "childish ways" you wish you could "put behind you" right now? (Responses might include: "I still throw temper tantrums"; "I get nervous talking to people of the opposite sex"; "My mom still chooses all my clothes"; "I don't know how to do my hair or make-up"; "I don't know how to cook—even simple things"; "I never have any money," etc.)

What are some things you hope *won't* change when you get older? (Responses might include: "I still want to be happy"; "I still want to have a lot of friends," etc.)

Say: **This worksheet illustrates how you are right in the middle of some very key changes. You aren't really a child, but you're not really an adult yet, either. It's a tough time—no denying. You feel that you deserve a little more respect and that you are sometimes treated like a child.**

3 "I Don't Get No Respect"

Have the kids sit in a circle. Take out a lump of Play-Doh and manipulate it with your hands in some way to show disrespect (maybe slap it or smash it). Say: **I don't get any respect when . . .** and then share an area where you feel you don't get the respect you deserve.

Then toss the Play-Doh gently to a teen sitting in the circle. Instruct him or her to manipulate the clay to show disrespect and to name an area where he or she "gets no respect." (Examples might include: "When Mom and Dad and I are arguing and they dismiss everything I say as 'backtalk'" or "When my teacher embarrasses me in front of the whole class.") Give everyone a chance to contribute.

Then say: **Well, there seem to be many ways that we're not respected. Remember what you said, and when we pass the Play-Doh around again, manipulate it in some way to show respect. Then tell us how you think respect could have been shown to you in the situation you named earlier.** (Examples might include: "I just wish my parents would listen—they don't even have to agree" or "My teachers could show respect for my feelings and discipline me in private.") Again, give everyone a chance to contribute.

4 The Carpenter's Son

Distribute copies of "The Carpenter's Son" (Student Sheet 8-B). Have kids read the "diary entry" and complete the questions at the bottom of the sheet. When everyone is finished, discuss the kids' responses using the following information.

1. How do you feel when you think about Jesus once being your age? ("Gives me something new to think about"; "Encourages me"; "I'd never really thought about it before.")

2. *What are some keys for gaining the respect of others?* (Behaving responsibly; having a strong sense of responsibility; having a desire to please God, parents, and others.)

3. *What are some areas of responsibility in your life that you could learn to handle better to change how older people view you?*

"To gain the respect of my parents and change their view of me I need to ..." ("Be more responsible with the things they ask me to do"; "Communicate with them better," etc.)

"To gain the respect of other people and change their view of me I need to ..." ("Be respectful"; "Be more responsible," etc.)

Say: **I Timothy 4:12 says, "Don't let anyone look down on you because you are young, but set an example for the believers in speech, in life, in love, in faith and in purity."**

Basically it is saying, "Give people living examples of how grown-up you are." In this case it was encouraging Timothy specifically to let Christ shine through his life in speech, life, love, faith, and purity as proof of his maturity. Maturity needs to be proved to change the views of those who are older than you.

Using this passage as our guide, let's brainstorm some ideas of how we can change society's view of us, or how we can "set an example for the believers in speech, in life, in love, in faith and in purity." List these five areas on the board and enter your group members' suggestions. The following are some suggested answers for each area:

Speech—Watch your words; don't gossip; don't cut others down; don't harm another with your words; be an encourager; compliment others.

Life—Live righteously; serve others; avoid bad company; hang around people who behave positively; try to behave responsibly; follow Christ at home; be committed to friendships.

Love—Be kind; be loving; be caring; be patient; love unconditionally.

Faith—Pray; know God's Word; show your faith by your deeds (service/caring); maintain a regular devotional/prayer time; share your faith.

Purity—Avoid rebellion; test everything; avoid evil; flee youthful lusts; don't hate; don't look down on others; think on good things; confess your sins; seek forgiveness from those you hurt; work to be like Christ.

Discuss your kids' ideas. Then ask your kids to seriously consider incorporating some of the ideas into their lives. Point out again how seeing responsible behavior causes people to change their views of others. A mature reputation must be *earned.*

Close the session in prayer, asking God for His wisdom and guidance for the kids struggling to change older people's opinions of them.

Option for Use in Youth Group

King/Queen for the Day

Select one of your group members in advance to get the "royal treatment." At the beginning of the meeting, bring the person out in front of the rest of the kids and introduce him or her as "King" or "Queen" for the day.

Have the King/Queen sit in a special chair (perhaps even decorated). Bring him or her special food and snacks; do the things he or she asks you to do; let him or her order you around, etc.

After a few minutes of this, ask the rest of the group:

What special treatment would you ask for if you were in this position?

What should this person be thankful for?

How would it feel if you were King or Queen?

When you're finished, contrast the "royal treatment" received by the King/Queen with the disrespect that young teens often receive in society.

Ask: **Wouldn't it be nice to be treated specially by your teachers, parents, and other adults?**

Wouldn't it be nice just to be treated as "one of them"?

Adapting the Session for Sixth Graders

Simplify Student Sheet 8-A by changing the second section to "Now," rather than "When I Become an Adult." Change the first question in the discussion to "How much is different in your life from five years ago?" You may also want to skip the "I Don't Get No Respect" exercise and instead use the "King/Queen for the Day" exercise.

When I Was a Child — When I Become an Adult

Finish the thoughts for the "When I was a child" section. Then use your imagination to complete the "When I Become an Adult" section.

When I was a child (five or so years ago), I . . .

looked . . .
loved . . .
wore . . .
thought . . .
laughed at . . .
was best friends with . . .
was afraid to . . .
was good at . . .
thought of God as . . .
cried when . . .
listened to . . .
played with . . .
never . . .
was not allowed to . . .
had a problem with . . .
was happiest when . . .
didn't know . . .

When I become an adult (10 years from now), I will . . .

look . . .
love . . .
wear . . .
think . . .
laugh at . . .
be friends with . . .
be afraid to . . .
be good at . . .
think of God as . . .
cry when . . .
listen to . . .
play with . . .
never . . .
be allowed to . . .
have a problem with . . .
be happiest when . . .
not know . . .

The Carpenter's Son

Read the following diary entry and answer the questions that follow on your own.

Dear Diary,

It's great working with the best carpenter in town. Everybody wants our woodwork. Around here I have learned that the highest honor a son can pay his father is to learn his father's craft and perform it with comparable quality. I have noticed that, because of our quality work, I often hear the adults complimenting both Joseph and me. This brings me great joy, for I share the same love for carpentry.

Today was a very busy day. I did my chores, took care of my clothes and bed, helped with my brothers, worked in the carpenter's shop, and many other things. It's interesting that many other young men I know who are my age don't seem to want to do these things, and complain. They don't fully understand that this is good for them and will help them learn responsibility and become mature. They still behave like children, so they should not be shocked when they are treated as children.

I love my home, and I love my Heavenly Father. I challenge myself every day to walk responsibly. I want to live a righteous life, and I believe the true test of this starts in our home. Those closest to me know if I am truly responsible or not, and my Heavenly Father sees everything. I have found that as a result of being responsible, my mother says things like, "Son, you are growing up quickly" and "You are a fine carpenter, young man." The rabbis and other adults I know speak to me as if I were an adult. Because of the respect I have for those at home and my Heavenly Father, I have gained their respect. This makes me joyful and I know it makes my Heavenly Father joyful.

I know that I will not be a carpenter forever. I'll still be a builder, but not of wood and stone. I have gained my Father's love for His craft. I'll remake people's lives.

Luke 2:52—"And Jesus grew in wisdom and stature, and in favor with God and men."

1. How do you feel when you think about Jesus once being your age?

2. What are some keys for gaining the respect of others?

3. What are some areas of responsibility in your life that you could learn to handle better to change how older people view you?

"To gain the respect of my parents and change their view of me I need to . . ."

"To gain the respect of other people and change their view of me I need to . . ."

Session 9

The onset of puberty can be a very frightening experience to a child who is not prepared for what is about to happen. In addition to the various biological changes and indications of sexual maturation, puberty is a period marked by numerous and complicated *developmental* tasks, particularly the need to adapt to various physical, psychological, and emotional changes.

Of course, it can also be a time of happiness and pleasure, of growing independence, of new and exciting ways of perceiving the world, and of satisfying social relationships.

As you lead this session, be aware that some of your group members are probably very sensitive about the changes they're experiencing, particularly the sexual changes. They will be especially attuned to your reaction to their questions and answers. Be sure not to use inappropriate humor, and don't make fun of their ideas.

[NOTE: It would be a good idea to give the parents of your group members advance warning of the sexual nature of this session's topic.]

A Whole New Set of Feelings

[Puberty]

What You Want to Do

- Help kids understand that God intricately designed the maturation process of our bodies;
- Help kids understand the physical and emotional implications of puberty;
- Help kids recognize the new responsibility they have to maintain sexual purity.

Where You'll Find Help

- Genesis 1:27
- Genesis 2:7, 22
- Psalm 139:13-16
- Psalm 145:17, 18
- Romans 8:35, 37-39
- I Corinthians 6:19, 20

What You'll Need

- Bibles
- Pencils
- Copies of "What's Good about Me"? (Student Sheet 9-A)
- Copies of "Girls' Puberty I.Q. Test" (Student Sheet 9-B)
- Copies of "Guys' Puberty I.Q. Test" (Student Sheet 9-C)
- Several newspapers
- Tape
- Dictionary
- An adult assistant (the opposite sex from yourself) to do the "Puberty I.Q. Test" with kids of the opposite sex

Cocoon

Ask: **How many of you have ever seen a butterfly? You may not know it, but that butterfly wasn't always a butterfly. It began as a caterpillar that crawled around eating leaves; then it encased itself in a cocoon; then it became a butterfly through a process called "metamorphosis." So the creature has to undergo two *big* changes before it becomes an adult butterfly.**

In the same way, you are about to begin, or have already begun, your own metamorphosis, called "puberty." There have probably been some real big changes going on in you and your body lately. And these changes will continue for the next few years. Today we're going to talk about these changes and find some encouragement for you in the Bible. To get you in the mood, let's play a game.

Divide the group into a girls' team and a guys' team. Instruct each team to choose one of its members to be a "caterpillar." Then have each team wrap its "caterpillar" in newspaper and tape so you can't see the person's clothing or skin at all. When the "caterpillars" are wrapped up in their "cocoons," they must hop 10 feet away. When they've done this, their teams can start tearing away the newspaper "cocoons." The "caterpillars" that were in the "cocoons" have now become "butterflies," so they must flap their wings (arms) and hop three times (as if they were flying). The team that completes this (and deposits all its papers into the trash) first is the winner. After the game, give the winning team a minute to celebrate.

Ask: **How did you feel during this exercise?**

In this exercise—and in real life—were the caterpillar and the butterfly separate creatures? (No. They are the same creature.)

Which is better looking to you—a caterpillar or a butterfly? (They will probably say the butterfly is better looking.)

In your opinion, which one is more beautiful to God? Point out that God sees the beauty in the caterpillar as well as the butterfly.

Say something like: **Maybe you feel like a caterpillar. But many of you, through no effort of your own, have begun to bloom into adulthood. You've begun puberty. Today we're going to talk about some of the changes you're experiencing, how you feel about yourself as you go through these changes, and what you can expect in the future.**

What's Good about Me?

Hand out copies of "What's Good about Me?" (Student Sheet 9-A). Say something like: **Some of the changes puberty brings can make you feel**

strange. Sometimes you'll probably feel ugly and wonder if you're normal or if you're growing ahead or behind people your age. You'll wonder if everything is going to turn out right. At other times you'll probably be confused by unusual thoughts that are coming into your mind. It's a tough time. And it's normal to have these concerns.

Have the kids complete Student Sheet 9-A. When they're finished, ask volunteers to share their responses to each question.

Ask: **How many of you thought this was difficult to do?** Probably quite a few of them found it difficult.

Of all the "good things" about you, which one is the best? Encourage several people to respond.

Puberty I.Q. Test

Distribute copies of "Girls' Puberty I.Q. Test" and "Guys' Puberty I.Q. Test" (Student Sheets 9-B and 9-C). You hand them out to those kids of your same sex; have your assistant hand the sheets out to the teens of your opposite sex.

Have the girls and guys separate into two parts of the room, or into separate rooms. Your assistant will lead the kids of his or her own sex, and you will lead kids of your same sex. Have the guys and girls complete the quizzes simultaneously.

When they're finished, read off the correct answers and have the kids grade their quizzes. Then add the total scores of all the guys and the total scores of all the girls. The team with the highest score wins.

The answers to the quizzes are as follows:

Girls' Puberty I.Q. Test—(1) B; (2) A; (3) B; (4) A; (5) A; (6) B; (7) B; (8) C; (9) B; (10) A.

Guys' Puberty I.Q. Test—(1) B; (2) A; (3) B; (4) A; (5) A; (6) A; (7) A; (8) C; (9) A; (10) C.

You may want to have a dictionary available to look up words on the quiz that kids have trouble with.

When the quizzes are finished, you and your assistant should be available to answer any questions kids may want to ask. Make sure you're both prepared for this. After the question time, reunite the girls and guys.

Say something like: **Some of you may be wondering if you're getting cheated in your physical development and appearance. It may seem to you like, somehow, God sneezed when you were coming down the line, and you missed out on good looks, body development, and a great personality. But let's look at the Bible—God's love letter to you and me—for some encouragement that God is in charge of our development and loves us very much.**

Biblical Assurance

Have the kids form six groups. Assign one of the following Scripture passages to each group. If you don't have enough kids for six groups, assign more than one passage to each group.

Instruct each group to:

- Find the main idea of its passage, as it relates to God's creation of us, His love for us, or our responsibility to keep ourselves pure from sexual sin.
- Determine how the passage relates to puberty.
- Decide how the passage can be an encouragement to someone going through puberty.

Give the kids about five minutes to work. Then have each group report its findings. The following are some possible answers to help you with the discussion.

Genesis 2:7, 22

Main Idea: God created Adam and Eve by His own hand and breath.

How It Relates to Puberty: The Creator of all things created us to change and grow.

Encouragement: God knows what He is doing; He is in control.

Genesis 1:27

Main Idea: God created us in His image, unlike any other created thing.

How It Relates to Puberty: God created my body, with all its changes, so each step must be right and good.

Encouragement: With God's help, I can make it through this.

Psalm 145:17, 18

Main Idea: God is righteous, loving, and near to us.

How It Relates to Puberty: I don't have to feel alone; God is with me.

Encouragement: I can always talk to God; He understands me and is near me.

Psalm 139:13-16

Main Idea: God used great detail in creating me and He knows me better than anyone else does.

How It Relates to Puberty: I'm not a mistake; nothing I need was left out.

Encouragement: God has all my changes planned out; I will turn out great.

Romans 8:35, 37-39

Main Idea: We can conquer anything that tries to separate us from God's love.

How It Relates to Puberty: I can handle any upsetting thing through Christ.

Encouragement: I can always count on God's love.

I Corinthians 6:19, 20

Main Idea: My body is a temple of God; I honor that fact by keeping myself sexually pure.

How It Relates to Puberty: I am to keep my new sexual feelings under control.

Encouragement: God wants me to have His best—whether it's sex in marriage, or a single life free from sexual sin.

Ask: **Which passage was most encouraging to you?**

How will these passages affect how you view yourself—changes and all—in the future?

Lead the group in a prayer of thanksgiving for a wise and loving Creator who has designed us uniquely. Thank God for specific good qualities mentioned about group members in this session. Pray that each teen would remember to turn to God at any time of need and to trust Him and His plan.

Option for Use in Youth Group

Another Metamorphosis Relay

Divide the group into four teams (with a mix of girls and guys on each team, if possible). Have the team members form four lines behind the first member in their team. Mark off a distance 15-20 feet away as the "end line." On the word "Go," the first person in each team moves to the end line and back using the "caterpillar" method. Then the other team members do the same, in relay fashion. When all the members of a team have completed the "caterpillar" method, they should then do the same thing, using the "butterfly" method. They continue until they have used all five methods of getting to the end line and back. The first team to complete all five methods wins.

The five methods are:

Caterpillar—Hold a chair between your knees as you walk, so six "legs" touch the ground.

Butterfly—Simulate flying by hopping and flapping your arms (wings).

Baby—Crawl on all fours.

Toddler—Walk heel to toe.

Adult—Broad jump to the end line; run back.

Adapting the Session for Sixth Graders

Alert parents to the content of this session. You may want to show them copies of the guys' and girls' quizzes to get their approval. You'll need to carefully explain some technical terms in this session. Other than that, however, this session should work well as written.

What's Good about Me?

One of the reasons puberty is such a tough time is that people change at different rates. As a result, you may be frustrated at times, or down on yourself. Save this sheet for the times when you're down or frustrated as a reminder that you're OK. Answer these questions and give yourself some encouragement and a few good pats on the back.

1. What's good about me physically?
(Example: I'm healthy; I can balance a lunchbox on my head, etc.)

2. What's good about me as a friend?
(Example: I'm loyal; I love to have fun, etc.)

3. What's good about me as a student?
(Example: I'm hardly ever absent; I'm really interested in history, etc.)

4. What's good about me as a Christian?
(Example: I want to know God better; I read my Bible, etc.)

5. What's good about me as a family member?
(Example: I don't give my brother as hard a time as he deserves; I still think my mom and dad are intelligent beings, etc.)

Girls'

Puberty I.Q. Test

Answer the following questions to the best of your ability. If you don't understand a word, just ask your leader for a definition. The highest total team score wins, so give it your best shot.

1. The point at which your body changes with the first signs of sexual maturity is known as _________.
A. adolescence B. puberty C. young life crisis

2. Girls reach physical maturity earlier than guys do. True or false?_________
A. true B. false

3. Which of the following glands causes acne? _________
A. pituitary B. sebaceous C. thyroid

4. Most people exhibit steady increases in motor-skill development (strength, reaction and coordination abilities). Which sex surpasses the other in this development? _________
A. guys surpass girls B. girls surpass guys

5. Many teens experience feelings of self-consciousness, shyness, and insecurity about the sexual changes that take place. A big factor that may produce self-consciousness is whether an adolescent is an *early* or *late* maturer. True or false? _________
A. true B. false

6. Before puberty, a rapid growth spurt occurs. For girls this usually happens between the ages of _________.
A. 17 and 18 B. 10 and 12 C. 13 and 15

7. Changes in the female body during adolescence are due largely to the presence of the hormone _________ in the female.
A. caffeine B. estrogen C. testosterone

8. Girls usually grow taller than boys between the ages of _________.
A. 10 and 11 B. 11 and 12 C. 11 and 13

9. Most girls will reach their maximum height at what age? _________
A. 15 B. 17 C. 19

10. Which of the following is mainly responsible for transforming a girl from her childish shape to a woman's shape? _________
A. sex hormones B. exercise and a good diet
C. widening of the pelvis

Guys' Puberty I.Q. Test

9-C

Answer the following questions to the best of your ability. If you don't understand a word, just ask your leader for a definition. The highest total team score wins, so give it your best shot.

1. The point at which your body changes with the first signs of sexual maturity is known as _________.
A. adolescence B. puberty C. young life crisis

2. Girls reach physical maturity earlier than guys do. True or false? _____________
A. true B. false

3. Which of the following glands causes acne? _________
A. pituitary B. sebaceous C. thyroid

4. Most people exhibit steady increases in motor-skill development (strength, reaction and coordination abilities). Which sex surpasses the other in this development? _________
A. guys surpass girls B. girls surpass guys

5. Many teens experience feelings of self-consciousness, shyness, and insecurity about the sexual changes that take place. A big factor that may produce self-consciousness is whether an adolescent is an *early* or *late* maturer. True or false? _________
A. true B. false

6. Before puberty, a rapid growth spurt occurs. For guys this usually happens betwen the ages of _________.
A. 10 and 16 B. 13 and 16 C. 11 and 14

7. Obvious bodily changes take place during the teen years, due largely to the presence of the hormone _________ in the male.
A. testosterone B. estrogen C. caffeine

8. At what age do guys usually enter into a period of rapid development? _____
A. 13 B. 14 C. 15

9. Which comes first, the ability to have a beard or a mustache? ______
A. mustache B. beard
C. both occur at the same time

10. Voice changes are due primarily to a rapid increase in _________.
A. the development of the larynx
B. the widening of the esophagus
C. the length of the vocal chords

Session 10

Spontaneous sexual thoughts, fantasy fragments, and sudden erotic impulses are exceedingly common for adolescents, especially for adolescent males. These feelings and thoughts are byproducts of healthy psychosexual development. But when these feelings and thoughts become the focus of attention, they can take the form of lustful fantasies, which are sinful. Junior highers need to learn to deal with sexual urges without allowing them to become sin.

Your group members need to recognize that God's plan for sex—*two* people expressing their love within marriage—is much more satisfying than the "cheap thrills" of temporarily giving in to lust. They also need to know that God is willing to help them when they are tempted.

Be sure to notify in advance the parents of your group members as to the nature and content of this session.

Runaway Thought Life

[Lust and Masturbation]

What You Want to Do

- Help kids realize that if they follow God's plan for sex—*two* people expressing their love within marriage—they will enjoy it much more than if they give in to their lust;
- Help kids understand that God is willing to help them when they are tempted by lust.

Where You'll Find Help

- II Samuel 11:1–12:25
- Psalm 119:9-11
- Proverbs 19:20
- Matthew 5:27, 28
- Philippians 4:8
- II Timothy 2:22
- James 5:16
- I John 1:9

What You'll Need

- Bibles
- Pencils
- Copies of "The Lie of Lust" (Student Sheet 10-A)
- Copies of "Mind Guard Deodorant" (Student Sheet 10-B)
- Markers
- White poster board cut into signs
- Tape
- Paper
- An adult of the opposite sex to help with "Randy's Story" or "Rachel's Story"
- A copy of "Randy's Story" or "Rachel's Story" for your assistant

1

Sex! Sex! Sex!

Before the session, cut a few sheets of white poster board into 10-20 small signs. Write the word "Sex" on each sign. Post the signs around the room.

Begin the session by asking: **Does anything about the room jump out at you?** (Sex.)

Sometimes it seems like you're surrounded by sex—in advertising, on TV, in the clothes people wear and the things they talk about.

What kinds of problems might be caused by being surrounded by reminders of sex all the time? (It could begin to plant sexual thoughts in our heads.)

Say something like this, if it applies to you: **When I was your age, I used to think about sex a lot. At times I still do. If you haven't begun to think a lot about sex yet, you probably will very soon. It's something we all have to deal with at one time or another. Today we're going to talk about sexual thoughts that become a problem and lead us to sin.**

2

Is It Lust?

Say something like: **In Matthew 5:27, 28, Jesus says, "You have heard that it was said, 'Do not commit adultery.' But I tell you that anyone who looks at a woman lustfully has already committed adultery with her in his heart."** (You might want to explain that "lust" in this passage refers to wrong sexual thoughts, while "adultery" implies wrong sexual activity.) **Keep these verses in mind. When I read the following situations, I want you to react in one of three ways:**

- ***Stay seated* if you feel the person in the example *hasn't* begun to lust;**
- ***Stand up* if you feel the person *has* begun to lust;**
- ***Wave your arms* if you feel the person is lusting *big time*.**

Read the following examples and wait for group members to respond.

1. Sue is watching her favorite soap opera when a steamy love scene comes on. Instead of turning the channel, Sue watches the scene all the way through. Has Sue begun to lust?

2. While paying for a candy bar at a convenience store, Joey noticed the cover of one of the pornographic magazines behind the counter. Now he can't get that picture out of his mind. Has he begun to lust?

3. As Matt is telling Rick a dirty joke, Rick begins to get some explicit pictures in his mind. Has Rick begun to lust? What about Matt?

Ask: **Which of the examples did you find most difficult to decide on?**

Say something like: **Some of you have already begun to start thinking more about sex; that's only natural. But how do you know when sexual thoughts become sinful?** (When you dwell on the thought and let it progress;

when you act on the thought; when your conscience convicts you, etc.)

Say: **There's an old saying that goes something like this: "You can't stop the birds from flying over your head, but you can keep them from making a nest in your hair." How does this apply to impure sexual thoughts that might pop into our minds?** (If an impure sexual thought just pops into your mind, it's not your fault—just like the birds flying over your head, there's nothing you can do about it; but if you choose to dwell on the thought and act on it—if you allow it to "build a nest"—it can become sin.)

3 The Lie of Lust

Say something like: **God's plan for sex is *two* people expressing their love for each other within marriage. Looking at someone lustfully twists God's plan because it's selfish; it involves only one person thinking about what another person could do for him or her sexually. You need to be aware of this as you experience more and more sexual thoughts.**

Let's look at one person in Scripture who chose to pursue his lust and the terrible sin that resulted.

Hand out copies of "The Lie of Lust" (Student Sheet 10-A). Have kids read the account of David. Then discuss as a group the questions that follow. Avoid pushing kids to be too specific if they are not comfortable talking about sex.

Ask: **What was David's first mistake?** (Looking at naked Bathsheba long enough to want to find out who she was.)

Why didn't David ask God's forgiveness earlier for what he was doing? (He had chosen the easy way to deal with his temptation—he acted on it. Then sin clouded his mind and he picked what he saw as the easy way out—having Uriah killed.)

How would asking God earlier for forgiveness have saved him? (If David had asked God's forgiveness for his lust, Uriah would have lived, and David's house would have remained peaceful. Everyone might have lived happily ever after.)

How was David's act self-centered? (He was thinking only about a night of sex for him. He didn't think about the harm it would cause his family and Bathsheba's marriage.)

David had many wives; how did he step outside of God's plan by getting involved with Bathsheba? (God's plan for sex is two people expressing love *within marriage;* the sex between David and Bathsheba occurred outside of marriage. David also didn't trust God to help him with his temptation.)

Say: **As you can see, lust can lead to some pretty bad results. You're probably beginning to understand that God's plan for sex is exciting, pleasurable, and carefree. Stepping outside of God's plan leads to fear, heartache, and destruction.**

A Problem Related to Lust (optional)

Say something like: **There's a topic related to lust that we need to talk about today. But we're going to talk about it in different groups.** Separate the girls and guys for this activity (if possible, use separate rooms). You will lead the discussion for the kids of your same sex and your assistant will lead the discussion for kids of the opposite sex.

The guys should be read "Randy's Story" and the girls should be read "Rachel's Story." Feel free to change the wording of the stories to fit your group, your church, and your own sensitivities.

Randy's Story

Randy is 13. He's an average guy, well-known and well-liked at school. Recently Randy's body has begun to develop in some surprising ways. And he's noticed that some of the girls around him have been growing up, too. He's been troubled lately because of his thoughts. He can't seem to control the ideas and images that pop into his mind. He's also been troubled by something he's been doing when he's alone as a result of his thoughts.

Lately, when he thinks about sex, he also touches himself in ways that imitate having sex. In other words, he masturbates. One of his friends told him about it one day, so he tried it. Now he's sorry he did. He feels strange in his room alone thinking up things in his mind and masturbating.

"Is this wrong to do, or am I OK?" he asks. He feels very guilty and wonders, *Am I normal?*

When you've finished the story, say something like: **On the back of your worksheet, I want you to write "yes" or "no" to the following questions:**

Is Randy normal?

Should he feel bad or guilty about masturbating?

Is this lust?

Rachel's Story

Rachel is 13. She's an average girl, well-known and well-liked at school. Her body has begun to develop in some surprising ways recently, just like some of the other girls. Rachel has also noticed that guys seem to be more interesting to her lately. All these changes seem strange and new to her.

Some things have been happening lately that are even more confusing to Rachel. Her friends have been talking a lot about sex. One of her friends even claims to have done it, which really surprised Rachel. Rachel is starting to think about sex a lot and what it would be like. Sometimes really graphic thoughts strike her at strange times. She wonders if she's weird or something.

Another friend has told Rachel about things she does to herself to find out what sex feels like. That surprised Rachel as well. Last week Rachel got so curious about sex that she tried to find out what it felt like by stimulating herself. In other words, she masturbated. Then a few days later she did it

again.

Now Rachel feels guilty. She knows that runaway sexual thoughts can lead to sin. She's really been battling with this. She wonders, *Am I lusting?* and *Is this wrong?*

Say something like: **On the back of your worksheet, I want you to write "yes" or "no" to the following questions:**

Is Rachel normal?

Should she feel bad or guilty about masturbating?

Is this lust?

[NOTE: The following teaching responds to these issues. Teach it as written or use your own material. But avoid raising issues that you cannot deal with.]

Talk frankly with your kids about masturbation. Point out several things:

1. It's something that just about everybody does at one time or another.

2. Some girls as well as guys do it.

3. You're not "weird" for doing it.

4. Christians disagree over how or whether the Bible talks about this subject. But most would say the thoughts that accompany it often are sinful.

5. Masturbation is a totally self-centered act and can cause an attitude of self-centeredness about sex.

6. Any excessive guilt or shame you feel concerning masturbation may cause you severe distress. If so, see a mature counselor you know and trust and confide in him or her. Don't carry the burden alone.

Be sure to offer the counsel of yourself and your assistant to any group members who need to talk.

5 Mind Guard Deodorant

Say something like: **Suppose someone had discovered a mind "deodorant" that was able to completely erase excessive sexual thoughts by just being sprayed on a person's forehead.**

Hand out copies of "Mind Guard Deodorant" (Student Sheet 10-B). Explain the directions to the kids. Then give them about 10 minutes to complete the sheet. When they've finished, go over the "Secret Ingredients of Mind Guard" with them.

Point out that no mind deodorant will ever be produced. But God has given us guidance and power to resist runaway thoughts through His Word, through prayer, and through the wise counsel of adults.

Emphasize how I John 1:9 shows God's willingness to help us when we are tempted. Then close the session in prayer, asking God for His help for kids who may be struggling with sexual thoughts.

Option for Use in Youth Group

Object Pass

Have everyone form a circle. Give each person an object, which can be large or small, and of any shape (such as a chair, a book, a piece of paper, a pencil, shoe, a purse, etc.). Each time you say "Go," have everyone pass his or her object to the right—using only one hand. The objects must keep moving at all times. When a person drops an object, he or she must leave the game; but his or her object remains. As the game progresses, there quickly remain more objects in the game than people, making it harder and harder to avoid dropping an object. The winner is the last person to avoid dropping an object.

After the game, ask: **How did you feel during the game?**

What was the toughest part of this game?

Point out that, at times, everyone feels overwhelmed (like in the game you just played). We feel overwhelmed when we are put in a position where we have to handle things that we don't feel capable of handling. One area that can be overwhelming is our sexual thought life. At times the thoughts come so fast and furiously that it's hard to stay pure in our thinking.

Explain that God has some excellent truth in His Word to help us to deal with our runaway thoughts.

Adapting the Session for Sixth Graders

If you or the parents of your kids decide that it is inappropriate for 12 year olds to discuss masturbation, leave out any mention of masturbation as you and your assistant read Rachel's and Randy's stories. Discuss only the issues of lust and growing sexual realization.

Or you could leave out Rachel's and Randy's stories and just do the "Mind Guard" exercise, again emphasizing the kids' growing sexual realization.

The LIE of Lust

10-A

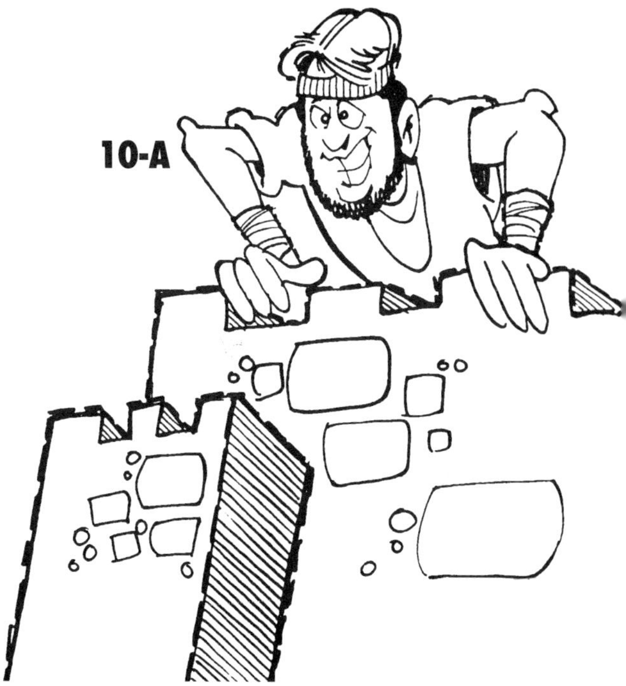

One night King David was walking around on the roof of his palace when he saw a beautiful woman bathing. After inquiring, he found out that she was Bathsheba, the wife of one of his personal bodyguards. He sent for her and she came to him. He went to bed with her, then sent her back home.

After a short time, she reported to David that she was pregnant. Because her husband had been away at war, everyone would know her husband wasn't the father of her baby. David called her husband, Uriah, back from war to go to bed with his wife. Uriah refused out of respect for his fellow soldiers who were still at war.

This put David in a jam. He sent Uriah back to the war, and ordered that Uriah be put in a position where he would most likely be killed in battle. It worked. Uriah was killed, and David promptly married Bathsheba.

David's actions greatly displeased the Lord. The Lord sent Nathan the prophet to David. Nathan told David a story about a rich man who owned many sheep and cattle, and a poor man whose only possession was one lamb. One day, the rich man wanted to prepare a meal for a guest. But rather than using one of *his* many sheep, the rich man stole the poor man's only lamb.

David was very angry when he heard Nathan's story and declared that the rich man should die. Nathan replied, "You are the man!" He went on to explain how David had many wives, and how David still wasn't satisfied. Instead, David had taken the only wife of Uriah—and then had Uriah killed.

As Nathan spoke, David realized he had greatly sinned before the Lord.

The child Bathsheba bore to him died a few days later as punishment from God, which greatly distressed David. The Lord also warned David that fighting would be brought to his household as a result of his sin. (Adapted from II Samuel 11:1–12:25)

What was David's first mistake?

Why didn't David ask God's forgiveness earlier for what he was doing?

How would asking God earlier for forgiveness have saved him?

How was David's act self-centered?

David had many wives; how did he step outside of God's plan by getting involved with Bathsheba?

Mind Guard Deodorant 10-B

Keep that mind fresh all day long! Just spray a little "Mind Guard Deodorant" on your forehead to get rid of excessive or wrong sexual thoughts.

Create a slogan for this product. Then look at the secret ingredients and Scripture references to find the real "mind guard" God has given us.

SLOGAN: (Example: "Fresh relief for an odorous mind!")

____

Secret Ingredients of Mind Guard!

1. When you catch your mind going astray into impure thoughts, immediately replace them with pure thoughts. (Read Philippians 4:8.)

2. Avoid sexually stimulating magazines, movies, videos, jokes, songs, books, etc. (Read II Timothy 2:22.)

3. If you feel controlled by sexual thoughts, seek wisdom from a trusted counselor.
(Read James 5:16 and Proverbs 19:20.)

4. Seek God's power and help in rescuing you.
(Read Psalm 119:9-11.)

REMEMBER: God is always willing to help you when you are tempted by lust—even if you've given in to lust before.

"If we confess our sins, he is faithful and just and will forgive us our sins and purify us from all unrighteousness"
(I John 1:9).

Session 11

You see it in the advertisements for a popular sports magazine's annual "swimsuit issue." You see it in the previews for Hollywood's highest-grossing movies. Our society seems to be in a constant state of sexual hysteria; people can't seem to see or hear enough about it. At least the media "powers that be" are convinced of this. Sex is splashed across all forms of media to get people to buy everything from cars to perfume.

Many rock music performers deify sex. Even love songs by "clean-cut" rock groups are often little more than hormonal moanings of sexual innuendo ("Ooh, baby, you got what I need"). And how many music videos have you seen that *didn't* use half-naked women or hints of sexual perversion to get their messages across?

Because our society lacks restraint, kids are bombarded with concentrated mega-doses of sexual information (mostly false and usually twisted) from every form of media: TV, movies, songs, music videos, magazines, etc. Add to this the fact that kids are much more independent and unsupervised today, and it is obvious that they must learn responsibility in the area of guarding themselves against this sexual barrage. They must also learn how to discern the amount and content of the entertainment and advertising they should experience.

Life in a Sexual Society

[Media]

What You Want to Do

- Help kids identify specific areas of society that cause them to be sexually tempted;
- Help kids brainstorm God-honoring ways to avoid tempting situations;
- Help kids commit to eliminating as much sexual temptation in their lives as possible.

Where You'll Find Help

- I Thessalonians 5:21, 22
- I Corinthians 6:18

What You'll Need

- Bibles
- Pencils
- Copies of "Sex and the Media" (Student Sheet 11-A)
- Copies of "Three Kids and the Media" (Student Sheet 11-B)
- Chalkboard and chalk
- Markers

1 Foot Media

Say something like: **Imagine you are on a planet where the inhabitants' bodies look like human feet, with their faces located near the toes. The media people on this planet, who want to make big bucks by pushing their products, have decided that the way to get to people's hearts, and money, is to use feet.**

Divide the kids into four groups and assign each group one of the following products to advertise in a TV commercial. In the commercials, group members may only use their feet and voices (or any props they can hold with their toes). Everyone in each group must be involved as either a "foot actor," an artist (drawing on the actors' feet), or a writer.

Here are some suggested products to advertise:

- Dr. Toes' Anti-Fungal, New, Improved Foot Powder (with perfume scent)—"Tired of that fungus rotting your toenails off? Well . . ."
- Rich Persimmons' Guaranteed Foot Weight Loss Plan—"Tired of those unsightly chubby toes? Well . . ."
- Bald Eagle Miracle Toe and Foot Hair Implants and Removal—"Hair on top of your toes and feet got you down? Need more? Well . . ."
- Sandpaper Cream Bunion Treatment and Preventative—"Bunions giving you a toe-ache, making you feel strange in the crowd? Well . . ."

Give the groups several minutes to work; then have them present their commercials. Afterward, discuss the activity, using the following questions.

On this imaginary planet, the media used feet to sell products. What does the media in our society use to sell products? (The answer you're looking for is "sex.")

Why do you think using sex or sex appeal is effective in advertising? (Sex is attention-getting.)

Why do you think sex attracts people's attention so easily? (Because most people think about sex quite a bit.)

Would an advertisement using sex or sex appeal get *your* attention? Why or why not? Maintain an accepting, non-judgmental attitude toward volunteers' responses. Encourage your group members to be honest.

What are some other forms of media that use sex to get people's attention? (TV, radio, movies, music videos, music, newspapers, etc.)

Say something like: **At your age, you're probably thinking about sex more than ever before. For the first time in your life, you're experiencing serious sexual temptation. And the sexual information you're getting from all the different kinds of media increases your temptation. So obviously, a way to cut down on your sexual thoughts is to control the amount and the kind of media input you get.**

Messages of the Media

Say: **Let's talk about some of the sexual messages you've gotten from some songs you've listened to and some music videos and movies you've seen.**

Ask kids to give you some specific examples of songs, music videos, and movies that contain sexual messages. Enlist three volunteers (one for songs, one for videos, and one for movies) to write the examples on the board as they're given. Suggest a few examples of your own to get kids started. Again, maintain a non-judgmental attitude as kids offer examples. You want them to be honest, and not worry about your reaction to what they say.

After you've received several examples, write the following messages on the board:

A. Lust is love.

B. Sex is love.

C. Sex is a good basis for relationships.

Ask: **Do you believe any of these statements? Why or why not?** Allow time for brief response.

Do you know of anyone who believes any of these statements? Emphasize that you're not looking for *names* of people here. You're just trying to help group members recognize that these beliefs are prevalent in today's society.

If possible, have kids match one of these three messages with the sexual messages found in some of the songs, videos, and movies they listed.

Say: **The media throw a lot of bad information at us. As far as sex is concerned, the messages of the media often say one of these three things: (A) Lust is love; (B) Sex is love; and (C) Sex is a good basis for relationships. Because the media offer ideas like these about sex, it's important that you learn to control the media you experience.**

How much media and sexual content are you exposed to? Let's take a quiz to find out.

Sex and the Media

Hand out "Sex and the Media" (Student Sheet 11-A). Instruct kids to fill out the quiz. Give them five minutes to complete it. When time is up, read off the following answers and see how well everyone did. Allow time for discussion of the questions and answers.

Sex and the Media Answer Key

(1) D—1,300. (According to a study in *Christian Home & School.)*

(2) A—1,500. (According to a study in *Christian Home & School.)*

(3) D—15,000. (According to Zondervan Publishing House.)

(4) C—2. (According to a policy statement of the American Academy of Pediatrics.)

(5) B—41%. (According to a Louis Harris poll for Planned Parenthood, 1986. Reported in *American Teens Speak: Sex, Myths, TV and Birth Control.*)

(6) C—36.6%. (According to a Teenage Research Unlimited Syndicated Study, 1986.)

(7) D—Movies. The other choices appear in descending order. (According to a Josh McDowell Ministry survey, 1987. Reported in *Teen Sex Survey in the Evangelical Church: Executive Summary Report.*)

(8) A—94%. (According to the *Journal of Communication.*)

(9) D—R. (According to a Josh McDowell Ministry survey, 1987. Reported in *Teen Sex Survey in the Evangelical Church: Executive Summary Report.*)

(10) D—48%. (According to Teenage Research Unlimited Syndicated Study, 1986.)

Ask: **Which answer or statistic was most surprising to you?**

How do you feel after taking this quiz and learning this information?

How do you think a Christian should respond to all this? Give the kids time here. This is a necessary transition to the next activity.

4 Media Response

Distribute copies of "Three Kids and the Media" (Student Sheet 11-B). Have the kids form three groups. Assign each group one of the approaches on the worksheet. Have each group work together to find the strengths and weaknesses of its assigned approach. Give the groups 5-10 minutes to complete the assignment.

When all the groups have finished, ask a spokesperson from each group to report its findings.

Then ask: **Which of these approaches do you personally agree with? Why?** Encourage several group members to respond.

5 The Overriding Principle

Ask a volunteer to read aloud I Corinthians 6:18.

Say something like: **Some passages in the Bible instruct us to stand firm against temptation. Why do you suppose this one tells us to "flee"?** (Sexual temptation is so dangerous that the best way to fight it is to get away from it.)

Is it possible to get away from sexual temptation all together? No.

Is it possible to cut down on the amount of tempatation we face? (Yes.)

Have each of the three groups look up the Scripture passage at the bottom of Student Sheet 11-B and brainstorm at least ten practical ways to lessen the intake of sexual information from the media. Give the groups a few minutes to work. Then have the spokespersons read their groups' lists.

Use the following to supplement the groups' suggestions: switching radio stations immediately when you hear a sexually explicit song come on; finding out whether a movie has sex scenes in it before you go see it; refusing to watch TV shows known for their sexual content, etc.

Write down all the suggestions on a master list. Then, if possible, make copies of the list and give them to your group members next week.

Close the session in prayer, asking God for His wisdom as your group members attempt to lessen the amount of sexual input they receive from the media.

Option for Use in Youth Group

Stop the Tape

You'll need a VCR and TV for this activity.

Before the session, record several TV commercials and clips of various TV shows and/or music videos. Play the tape during the session. Ask several volunteers to stop the tape whenever sexual references are made.

After viewing several sexual references in the commercials and clips, discuss with your group members how prevalent sex is in today's media.

Adapting the Session for Sixth Graders

Don't use the "Messages of the Media" and "Media Response" sections with sixth graders. Instead, discuss as a group "some things you've seen on TV and heard on the radio that go against God's ideas about sex." Also, don't split up into groups for "The Overriding Principle" section.

SEX and the MEDIA

11-A

1. In one year, the average teenage boy will witness _________ sexual acts or references on TV.
(A) 10,000 (B) 100 (C) 900 (D) 1,300

2. In one year, the average teenage girl will witness _________ sexual acts or references on TV.
(A) 1,500 (B) 1,700 (C) 100 (D) 900

3. Upon high school graduation, the average student has watched _________ hours of televi sion, compared to 12,000 hours spent in the classroom.
(A) 12,000 (B) 10,000 (C) 9,000 (D) 15,000

4. How many hours of rock videos does the average teen watch each day?
(A) 4 (B) 3 (C) 2 (D) 1

5. What percentage of teenagers thinks TV gives a realistic picture of pregnancy and the consequences of sex?
(A) 93% (B) 41% (C) 24% (D) 30%

6. What percentage of teenagers between the ages of 12 and 15 attend movies for 5 to 10 hours a week?
(A) 45.0% (B) 52.3% (C) 36.6% (D) 25.3%

7. Christian teenagers learn about sex mostly from their friends (38%), but the second most informative source (26%) is _________.
(A) parents (B) classes at school
(C) television (D) movies

8. Many teenagers watch soap operas. What percentage of the sexual encounters shown on soap operas happen between people who aren't married to each other?
(A) 94% (B) 81% (C) 22% (D) 44%

9. A survey of Christian teenagers showed that, of the movies they watch, 68% of them are rated _________.
(A) G (B) PG (C) PG-13 (D) R

10. What percentage of teenagers listen to the radio 11-20 hours a week?
(A) 35% (B) 69% (C) 11% (D) 48%

Three Kids and the Media

11-B

The "Boy in the Bubble" Approach

Tom, a Christian, is extremely concerned about keeping his mind and life pure before God. Therefore, he's also extremely concerned about the sexual content in the media. His advice is "Turn it off!"

Tom never watches TV or movies, never listens to the radio, and never reads magazines or books (other than the Bible and those books he must read for school). He gets upset when he's around people who talk about the sex they see or hear in the media. He often tells them to "clean up their act." This is tough for Tom, but he feels that one day he will be rewarded for his purity and his separation from sex in the media.

Strengths of this response:____

Weaknesses of this response:____

The "If You Can't Beat 'Em, Join 'Em" Approach

Sue is a Christian who just tries to do the best she can. She doesn't see why she should miss out on all the great new movies and songs on the radio just because they sometimes talk about sex. Her advice is "Don't worry about it—enjoy!"

Sue knows that other Christians see problems with this, but she doesn't feel it's such a big deal. She watches all the latest movies and listens to all the newest songs. She reads magazines to find out how to make boys notice her and how to do her hair and make-up. She would never think of telling people to "clean up their act." As a matter of fact, she often listens to her friends talk about sex and learns from them. Sue is convinced that God wants her to have a good time.

Strengths of this response:____

Weaknesses of this response:____

The "Trying to Keep a Balance" Approach

Sam is a Christian. He wants to have a pure mind and live in a way that pleases God. He examines the media by asking himself, "Would Jesus watch, listen to, or read this?" His advice is "Watch, read, and listen, unless it gets trashy."

Sam goes to movies occasionally, but avoids the ones with obscene language and stupid ideas about sex. He listens to the radio, but changes the station if a song starts giving him wrong ideas about sex. He often listens to Christian rock instead. He tries not to joke about sex with his friends and prays for God's power to keep him from temptation. He has also memorized some Bible verses to stay disciplined and to keep from thinking about sex all the time and in the wrong way.

Strengths of this response:____

Weaknesses of this response:____

Media Monitor

Look up the following Scripture passage. Then come up with at least 10 practical ways to lessen the amount of sexual input you get from the media.

I Thessalonians 5:21, 22: "Test everything . . . Avoid every kind of evil." (Examples: Avoid looking at any kind of pornography; stop renting R-rated videos, etc.)

Session 12

A recent survey found that the four biggest reasons teenagers gave for having premarital sex were:

- Peer pressure—30%
- Curiosity—15%
- "Everybody's doing it!"—12%
- "Boys pressuring girls into it"—9%.

The same survey reported that the sexual experience of teens increased rapidly with age. While just 4% of 12 year olds have had sex, the number jumps to 10% for 13 year olds and 20% for 14 year olds.

Many parents have begun to resign themselves to "current societal trends" and now expect, and even plan for, their children's sexual activity. So where can a teen turn for encouragement to remain sexually pure? To you (and your youth group or Sunday School class)?

This session is designed to help junior high kids understand the importance of holding out for God's best for sex—one partner, for life. But beyond this session, your kids need a voice of God's reason, someone to refute the messages of sexual pressure they receive every day and encourage them to remain pure. Will you be that person for them?

Experimentation Temptation

[Resisting "Finding Out What Sex Is Like"]

What You Want to Do

- Help kids understand that sex is a wonderful *wedding* gift from God, and that when it is used as He intended, it is the ultimate expression of love;
- Help kids understand that when sex is misused—even once—it spoils the joy of God's wedding gift.

Where You'll Find Help

- Genesis 24
- Genesis 29:18-21
- I Corinthians 6:18-20; 10:13
- Colossians 2:8
- Hebrews 13:4

What You'll Need

- Bibles
- Pencils
- Copies of "Jacob Can Wait" (Student Sheet 12-A)
- Copies of "Resist!" (Student Sheet 12-B)
- A pitcher containing two quarts of unsweetened Kool-Aid
- One cup of sugar

1

A Love Story

Ask for six volunteers to act in a skit. Explain that there are no lines to learn—all the actors have to do is follow your instructions as you narrate the story. Assign the roles of Isaac, Abraham, Abraham's servant, two Canaanite maidens, and Rebekah. (If you have fewer than six people in your group, you'll need to have kids play two or more roles.)

As you read the skit, use "dramatic timing" to allow the actors to perform the actions. Encourage your actors to "ham it up" in their performances.

A Love Story—Very *Loosely Based on Genesis 24*

Act 1

One day Isaac was walking in his father's field and singing, "Father Abraham had many sons, and many sons had Father Abraham . . ." when he slipped on some camel dung and fell down. He got up, then slipped again.

At that moment, two fair Canaanite maidens came to him, helped him up, and began pulling Isaac back and forth between them by his arms, crying, "Oh, Isaac, you hunk, come with me. Let's make beautiful music together." They pulled on Isaac some more—and some more.

Finally he broke loose and cried out, "Nay, verily, I say unto thee, you fair maidens are worshippers of idols."

He flung them away and dramatically jumped to the top of a chair and said, "I am saving myself for an Israelite wife."

Act 2

Abraham said to his servant, "Go find a wife for my son, Isaac. And if you fail, let me show you what might happen." Abraham ran at the servant, tackled him, then started messing up his hair.

After a few minutes, the servant ran out, jumped on his camel, circled around three times, and went forth. After the servant had gone a great distance, he stopped to rest at a well and prayed a serious prayer: "Lord, please bless my master and myself this day. Find him a wife who will bring water for me and my camel."

About this time, a beautiful maiden named Rebekah came forth with a large vessel for water balanced on her head. She was singing, "Father Abraham had many sons . . ." She greeted the servant. "Water for thee and thy camel, sir?" she asked sweetly.

"Sure, fill it up," he replied.

Rebekah climbed down into the well. When she was about halfway down, she slipped and fell into the water. She got up, filled the vessel with water, climbed back up, and gave the water to the servant. He drank some of the water and gave some to his camel.

"We're going to need more than this," he said. So Rebekah climbed down into the well again. And again she slipped and fell. She got up, filled the vessel with water, climbed back up, and gave the water to the servant. Again he drank some and gave some to his camel.

"I'm sorry," he said, "but my throat is still pretty dry. Could I have some more?" This time, to save time, Rebekah just jumped right into the well, filled the vessel with water, climbed back up, and gave the water to the servant.

At that moment, the servant cried, "I have found thee, the wife for my master!" Then he and Rebekah jumped on the camel and rode away.

Act 3

Isaac was nervously pacing in the field, talking to himself. "Will she be comely of appearance, not excessive of girth?" he asked himself. He struck a thoughtful pose. "Will she have a face like a camel?" he asked. He struck a thoughtful pose again. "Will she have kept herself pure as a wedding gift to me as I have done for her?" he asked.

Suddenly Isaac heard the servant shout, "Yo, Isaac, check this out!" The noise startled Isaac so much that he slipped in camel dung and fell down.

When Rebekah noticed Isaac, she became suddenly shy, whispering to herself, "I find him cute, much to my surprise."

Isaac got up from the ground, wiped himself off, and looked at Rebekah. Then he jumped on a chair again and dramatically said, "Thank You, God, for blessing me abundantly for my purity before You."

And everyone lived happily ever after.

When the skit is finished, give your actors a round of applause.

Explain to your group members that the skit was a humorous adaptation of a real Bible story. You might even want to read the actual account from Genesis 24, so group members won't be confused about what really happened.

Say something like: **Genesis 24:67 says, "Isaac brought her into the tent of his mother Sarah, and he married Rebekah. So she became his wife, and he loved her . . ." This story in Genesis 24 tells of trusting God's provision and timing, and of the beauty of sex in marriage.**

2 Jacob Can Wait

Distribute copies of "Jacob Can Wait" (Student Sheet 12-A). This worksheet examines briefly the biblical account of Jacob waiting and working for the honor of marrying Rachel.

Ask a volunteer to read this account (Genesis 29:18-21) from the worksheet. Then give group members a few minutes to answer the questions on the sheet. When everyone is finished, go over each question. Supplement your group members' responses with the following information.

Ask: **In your opinion, what is the best thing about Jacob's love?** (Jacob's love grew over time. This may have been the only "girlfriend" of his life. He was willing to wait for sex. Verse 20 says that the seven years "seemed like only a few days to him because of his love for her.")

What did this story say to you of Jacob's respect for himself and for Rachel? (He respected himself enough to remain sexually pure, and he respected and loved Rachel enough to wait for her.)

Was Jacob somehow superhuman to be able to resist having sex with Rachel for all those years? (No, in verse 21 he says, "Give me my wife. My time is completed, and I want to lie with her"—he was *very* human.)

How do you think Jacob was able to resist premarital sex with Rachel? (Probably in many of the same ways we do today. He avoided situations that could be too tempting; he had a deep sense of moral conviction; he had a strong relationship with God; he was self-controlled; he honestly loved Rachel.)

How can this encourage people today who would also like to remain sexually pure until marriage? (Jacob's story demonstrates that it can truly be done.)

Say: **It's tough to resist the pressure to have sex, but God will reward those who wait until marriage. Only the pure can fully know the pleasure and absolute joy of experiencing God's special *wedding gift* —sex in marriage with the one you've vowed to spend the rest of your life with.**

3 Missing Ingredient

Bring out a pitcher of unsweetened Kool-Aid. Ask: **Who wants something to drink?** Give a glass of Kool-Aid to everyone who asks for one. Wait for group members' reactions when they taste the unsweetened drink.

Ask: **What did you expect?** (A sweet drink.)

What did you get? (A bad-tasting drink.)

Why doesn't it taste like you expected it to taste? (It's missing an ingredient—sugar.)

Say something like: **Kool-Aid without sugar is like premarital sex. *Real* Kool-Aid has three ingredients: Kool-Aid, sugar, and water. *Real* sex—sex within marriage—also has three ingredients: the emotional ingredient, the physical ingredient, and the spiritual ingredient.**

The emotional ingredient is true love, commitment, and loyalty. The physical ingredient is pleasure and not having to worry about illegitimate pregnancy or sexual disease. The spiritual ingredient is two people becoming one.

You remember what the Kool-Aid with the missing ingredient tasted like. Premarital sex, which is also missing ingredients, is just as "sour."

Explain to your group members how each of the three ingredients of "real" (marital) sex is absent in premarital sex. Emotionally, the lifetime commitment of marriage is not present; physically, there is a high risk of illegitimate pregnancy and contracting a sexual disease; spiritually, instead of being an honorable sexual union that results in mutual pleasure and blessing, it becomes a joining of two people in sin.

4 Resist!

Distribute copies of "Resist!" (Student Sheet 12-B). Have the kids pair up and work on this sheet. When they are finished, have volunteers share their responses.

Use the following information to supplement their answers.

Colossians 2:8—Don't be a captive of false philosophies—like the idea that real sexual enjoyment can be had outside of marriage.

I Corinthians 6:18-20—Flee sexual immorality; your body is a temple of God; you are purchased, and are not your own; honor God with your body.

Hebrews 13:4—Decide that marriage is to be honored; God will judge the immoral.

I Corinthians 10:13—Many have been tempted as you are; God will not allow you to be tempted beyond what you can resist; you will have an escape.

Close the session in prayer, asking God to give your group members the strength to resist the temptation to "find out what sex is like." Also pray that the reward for their sexual purity would become a treasure to the Lord.

Option for Use in Youth Group

Leading the Blind

Ask a volunteer to leave the room. Outside the room, blindfold the volunteer. While the volunteer is out of the room, have the other kids set up an obstacle course, using the tables and chairs in the room. The obstacle course should be designed so that it leads in two directions.

Bring the blindfolded volunteer back into the room and instruct him or her to walk toward the sound of your voice. Instruct the other kids in the group to loudly yell false instructions to the blindfolded person to try to lead him or her *away* from you. The blindfolded person will not hear you; he or she will hear the rest of the group and be led to the wrong person.

Then send the blindfolded person out of the room again. Have the rest of the group rearrange the obstacle course, then repeat the process. This time, however, speak instructions a little more loudly to the blindfolded person. He or she may hear faint traces of your voice, but will probably still be misled.

Again send the blindfolded person out of the room, and repeat the activity. This time, however, enlist another teen to take hold of the blindfolded person's arm, whisper directions in his or her ear, and lead the person to you.

When the exercise is finished, ask the blindfolded person: **How did you feel the first time you made your way through the room?** (Confused.)

The second time? (Confused and frustrated.)

The third time? (Relieved and secure.)

What helped you the most? ("When the person took hold of my arm and led me to you.")

Say something like: **Along with the tempting voices in your head, there are some voices around you that will try to lead you astray, to get you to be sexually involved. These voices may come from your friends, or from the movies you watch, etc. But you are not alone in your challenge to resist sexual temptation. God is like the person who led the blindfolded person. He sees where we are and how we are being tempted. He offers us a way through all this sexual temptation so that, if we get married, we will be able to give and receive the best gift anyone can give another person—ourselves.**

Adapting the Session for Sixth Graders

In the "Jacob Can Wait" exercise, you may want to just read the sheet and explain or skip the phrase "lie with her." You may also want to leave out questions #2 and 4. Simplify the concepts in Step 3 by concentrating on one "missing ingredient" of premarital sex—the lifetime commitment that comes with marriage.

Jacob Can Wait

"Jacob was in love with Rachel [Laban's daughter] and said, 'I'll work for you seven years in return for your younger daughter Rachel.' Laban said, 'It's better that I give her to you than to some other man. Stay here with me.' So Jacob served seven years to get Rachel, but they seemed like only a few days to him because of his love for her. Then Jacob said to Laban, 'Give me my wife. My time is completed, and I want to lie with her' " (Genesis 29:18-21).

In your opinion, what is the best thing about Jacob's love?

What does this story say to you of Jacob's respect for himself and for Rachel?

Was Jacob somehow superhuman to be able to resist having sex with Rachel for all those years?

How do you think Jacob was able to resist premarital sex with Rachel?

How can this encourage people today who would also like to remain sexually pure until marriage?

Resist!

Look up the following passages and write down the advice each gives on how to resist sexual temptation.

Colossians 2:8

I Corinthians 6:18-20

Hebrews 13:4

I Corinthians 10:13

Session 13

One day while visiting a junior high school, I passed a group of young teenagers.

"OK, so it's set—Saturday morning we'll meet in the mall at the ice-skating rink around 10 o'clock," one girl said. She and the dozen or so junior high guys and girls gathered around her seemed pleased with the plan, and they all went their separate ways. These young teens probably didn't realize that their Saturday morning mall trip was putting them on the cutting edge of the current trend in dating—that is, "group dating." Just a few years ago, group dating was done almost exclusively by college students; then it became popular on high school campuses. Now it's catching on even among junior high teens.

However, when the topic of dating is brought up to young teens, they often think of it only in terms of "one-on-one" dating. In spite of the burgeoning group dating trend, recent statistics show that the average age of a teenage girl on her first "one-on-one" date is now 14 years old. Whether young teens have never dated, have dated only in a group setting, or have dated one-on-one, they should: know the purpose of dating; develop dating standards; and understand that dating demands responsibility.

What Age Is the Right Age?

[Dating]

What You Want to Do

- Help kids understand the tremendous amount of responsibility that goes with dating;
- Help kids identify reasons for dating;
- Help kids brainstorm God-honoring alternatives that would allow them to associate with the opposite sex in non-dating situations.

Where You'll Find Help

- Genesis 29:20
- I Corinthians 4:2; 6:18-20; 10:13; 15:33
- II Corinthians 6:14-16
- Ephesians 2:10; 6:2, 3
- Philippians 2:3, 4; 4:6, 7
- I Thessalonians 4:3-7

What You'll Need

- Bibles
- Pencils
- Copies of "A Look at Dating" (Student Sheet 13-A)
- Copies of "My Own Dating Rules" (Student Sheet 13-B)
- Paper
- Dating skit outlines written on index cards
- Tape

1 Dating: A Four-Part Drama

Before the session, write each of the following skit outlines on a separate index card.

To begin the session, have group members form four "skit teams." Give each team an index card with the team's assigned skit written on it. Allow several minutes for the teams to prepare their skits (which should run 1-3 minutes). Then have them present their skits one at a time.

(If your group is small, have the kids work together as one team. If yours is a one-sex group, bring an assistant of the opposite sex to play appropriate roles.)

The skit outlines are as follows:

Guy Calling Girl for First Date—Ted is really nervous talking to Sheila on the phone. He doesn't quite know how to ask her to meet him at the mall. Both Ted and Sheila have friends listening in who try to "help out." Show a believable ending.

Holding Hands at the Movies—Sally and Jerry are at a movie with two other couples. Sally and Jerry are both really embarrassed when they notice that the other couples are holding hands. Show how Jerry tries to be "cool" and hold Sally's hand, but finds many obstacles (like putting his hand in her Coke, spilling the popcorn, grabbing someone else's hand, etc.). End the skit any way you like.

Boy Meets Girl—Tim thinks he's pretty cool with the ladies. He spots the new girl, Jenny, with her friends. His friends challenge him to ask her to go to a movie with him. He accepts the challenge. How will the situation turn out?

First Date: The Whatta-You-Wanna-Do Blues—Two or three couples get in a car (driven by a parent). Each of them is excited about what they will do tonight, but everyone discovers that nobody has any idea where to go and what to do. They each had expected the others to have an idea. What ideas will they come up with? What will they end up doing?

When all the skits have been performed, give your actors a round of applause.

Then ask: **How might some of these skits have ended differently?** Allow time for a few responses.

What are some things about dating that you are most nervous about? Guys—is it asking the girls out? Girls—is it what kind of guys will ask you out? What is it that most concerns you? Allow time for plenty of response.

Say: **Many people—old and young—feel pressure in dating relationships because of all the responsibilities involved. For you, the pressure may be over whether to date at all. Or it may be about learning how dating works**

and what the various responsibilities are.

Your fears might be expressed in thoughts like: "How do I ask her to meet me at the movies?" "Should I bring a friend or not?" "Will he or she like me?" "What will we do?" "Where will we go?" "What will we talk about?" and "What should I wear?"

This may all seem overwhelming to you. You may not want to have anything to do with dating right now. In that case, you should know that it's good to just have fun with guys or girls you know in non-dating activities.

Let's brainstorm some non-dating alternatives that would allow you to just have fun with guys and girls.

2 The Brainstormathon

Instruct the kids to form two groups. Inform them that you're going to have a contest to see which group can come up with the most dating alternatives in five minutes. Explain that a dating alternative is an opportunity for guys and girls to do something together without having the responsibilities or pressures of dating.

Each group is to come up with dating alternatives in two categories: "Serving" alternatives, in which the activity benefits someone else; and "Just for Fun" alternatives, in which the activity is done simply to have a good time.

Have each group appoint two "recorders" to write down the group's ideas. Give each recorder paper and a pencil. Explain that one recorder is to list all the "Serving" dating alternatives and the other recorder is to list all the "Just for Fun" dating alternatives.

After the five minutes are up, have the recorders from each team read their teams' lists. The team with the most alternatives wins.

Supplement the teams' suggestions with the following:

"Serving" alternatives—Working in a soup kitchen; washing a car for parents or grandparents; singing at a nursing home; working with Special Olympics; participating in a March of Dimes walkathon; building a ramp for someone with a wheelchair; various church projects.

"Just for Fun" alternatives—Roller skating, bowling, basketball, volleyball, craftmaking, church activities, chaperoned parties with organized games, caroling, scavenger hunts, etc.

Ask: **Do you think it's possible to have fun doing a serving project together—say, like raking leaves for the elderly?** (This could be a lot of fun—clowning around, throwing leaves at each other, etc.)

Which of these ideas seem like the most fun to you? Encourage several group members to respond.

3 The Dating Life

Distribute copies of "A Look at Dating" (Student Sheet 13-A). Have kids fill out the "Essential Qualities of a Possible Date" section of the worksheet. Give them about a minute to do this. Then see which qualities kids selected in their top five by having them raise their hands as you go down the list. If any responses surprise you, ask the kids why they chose the qualities they did.

Ask: **Do you expect that the qualities you chose will change over time?**

Would you marry someone using the same qualities you chose for dating? Why or why not?

Read the following list of values. Have the kids give each statement a thumbs-up sign if they agree or a thumbs-down sign if they disagree. You may want to ask kids why they responded as they did to certain statements.

1. Any date could be a possible marriage partner.
2. The best age to begin dating is 13.
3. A Christian should never date a non-Christian.
4. Nobody should date around. Everyone should date only one person at a time.
5. If you are in love with someone, it's OK to touch that person sexually, as long as you don't have sex with him or her.
6. It's important to set standards for dating *before* your first date.
7. Christian dating should involve serving and helping others as well as enjoying ourselves.
8. If your parents don't approve of the person you're dating, you should stop seeing him or her.
9. As long as a Christian couple avoids drugs and sexual activity, they can do anything a non-Christian couple does on a date.

Ask: **How many of you have never really thought about some of these things before?**

How did you feel as you were responding to these statements? Encourage several group members to respond.

Say: **These statements deal with some of the responsibilities that go along with a dating relationship. A lot of responsibility goes with dating.**

4 Understanding Dating

Ask: **At what age should teenagers begin dating?** Encourage group members to try to reach some kind of consensus on an age.

Are people suddenly ready for dating the day they reach a certain age? Why or why not?

Do you think there's a better indicator than age to determine when someone is ready to date? Encourage suggestions from several kids.

Then suggest that there are four main indicators of whether or not someone is ready to date.

1. The person realizes that dating demands responsibility.
2. The person has a written list of dating standards he or she will stick to, even if it means losing some dates.
3. The person understands the purpose of dating.
4. The person has his or her parents' permission.

Instruct your kids to read the "Understanding Dating" section of Student Sheet 13-A. Then briefly go over the questions at the end of each account. Encourage several kids to respond to the questions.

Then distribute copies of "My Own Dating Rules" (Student Sheet 13-B). Ask group members to think about the standards on this sheet. Encourage them to look up the Scripture references and sign the sheet like a contract. Have volunteers share their responses.

Ask: **How do you feel about these standards?**

Have you ever thought this much about dating before?

What's the biggest thing you've learned about dating today?

Close the session in prayer.

Option for Use in Youth Group

Married Adults Dating Interview

Invite to your group two married couples—one with children in junior high or high school, and an elderly couple that has been married for a long time. Interview the couples about their dating and courtship.

You may want to supply the couples with copies of the following questions to get them ready for the interview, but inform them that the kids will add questions of their own.

Keep the interview to about 10 minutes. Here are some possible questions to ask:

1. What first interested you in your husband or wife?
2. What kinds of things did you enjoy doing when you dated/courted?
3. Describe your funniest date.
4. What was the most embarrassing thing to happen to you on a date?
5. What do you remember most about your first date?
6. What was your curfew and what did your parents not allow you to do?
7. Describe your first kiss together.
8. What was the most romantic thing your husband (then your boyfriend) did for you when you were dating?

Adapting the Session for Sixth Graders

Since twelve year olds have a longer wait for dating, they may not be very interested in the subject. Therefore, the following changes should be made to make the session more relevant to them.

Drop the skits at the beginning of the session, and go right to "Brainstormathon." Change "Essential Qualities of a Possible Date" on Student Sheet 13-A to "Essential Qualities of a Good Friend of the Opposite Sex." In the "Understanding Dating" section of Student Sheet 13-A, drop the questions that ask for "other responsibilities" and "other purposes" in dating.

A Look at Dating

Essential Qualities of a Possible Date

Select the top five qualities you would look for in a person to date. (1 = the first positive quality you would look for; 5 = the last positive quality you would look for.)

____ Good-looking
____ Has sense of humor
____ Strong Christian
____ Honest
____ Self-confident
____ Intelligent
____ Sensitive/kind
____ Liked by my parents
____ Makes conversation
____ Good manners
____ Respects me
____ Listens to me
____ Popular
____ Dates only me
____ Fun-loving

Understanding Dating

Read each of the following accounts and write down your reply to each question.

Pete's First Date

It's Pete's first date, and, boy, is it complicated. He never knew there were so many things to think about.

"Where will we go, what will we do? Will there be sexual pressure? How much money am I going to need? I wonder what kind of dad Sherry has. Will he like me? There's no way I can bring her home late, I know that. Oh, I have to remember to tell Mom and Dad where I'll be. So what am I going to wear?"

What are some of the responsibilities Pete has to deal with?

What other kinds of responsibilities does dating demand?

Jennifer: Dating with a Purpose

Jennifer has thought a lot about dating. She knows why her friends date—mainly to see what they can get from the other person. And it seems like a lot of the guys are after girls for sex.

Jennifer took a lot of notes in her youth group when they talked about dating. She's decided that some of the purposes for dating are: (1) so she can build friendships with guys and begin to understand them better; (2) so she and the guys she dates can serve others together; and (3) so she will know what qualities to look for in her future marriage partner.

In addition to Jennifer's list, what are some other possible purposes for dating?

My *Own* Dating Rules

Look at the following list and put an "x" in front of five dating standards you are going to work especially hard to follow in the next month—even if it means losing dates. Look up the Scripture references that follow the standards and challenge yourself to memorize them.

If you would like to commit yourself to these standards, sign your name at the bottom of the sheet as a contract with yourself.

____ 1. I will only date Christians because any date is a possible mate. (II Corinthians 6:14-16)

____ 2. I will not knowingly cause another person to fall into any sin (sex, drugs, etc.). (I Thessalonians 4:3-7)

____ 3. I will behave honestly and responsibly toward my parents by being home on time, introducing them to people I go out with, and letting them know what my plans are. (Ephesians 6:2, 3)

____ 4. I will stay away from getting sexually involved. (I Corinthians 6:18-20)

____ 5. If sexual temptation becomes overwhelming, I will stop dating to regain my self-control. (I Corinthians 10:13)

____ 6. I will not go to places that I know will tempt me to do the wrong thing (unchaperoned parties, sexy movies, etc.). (I Corinthians 15:33)

____ 7. I will use the dating relationship to serve and help others (assisting in a shut-in ministry, serving in a soup kitchen, etc.)—as well as to have a good time. (Ephesians 2:10)

____ 8. I will talk about my dating standards with a potential date before I agree to go out with the person, to make sure he or she agrees. (II Corinthians 6:14-16)

____ 9. My dating life belongs to God—I'll trust His direction. (Philippians 4:6, 7)

____ 10. I will always strive to treat my dates with consideration and respect. (Philippians 2:3, 4)

____ 11. If my parents do not approve of a person I date, I will value their opinion. (Ephesians 6:2, 3)

____ 12. I will not allow myself to be put in situations (parking, bad parties, being home alone with a date) where I would not live up to my dating standards . (I Corinthians 6:18)

____ 13. I trust God's timing for my dating. I won't rush into relationships. (Genesis 29:20)

____ 14. I will not waste big bucks on entertainment; I have to be wise in managing the money God provides me with. (I Corinthians 4:2)

I do hereby commit to the standards I have marked above—even if it means I date less than other people do.

Signed,

____

____

(Date)